M000096509

Enduring
Connections

The Columbia Partnership Leadership Series
from Chalice Press

www.chalicepress.com
www.thecolumbiapartnership.org

Enduring Connections

Creating a Preschool and Children's Ministry

JANICE HAYWOOD

Janice A. Haywood
Matthew 22:37-39

CHALICE PRESS

ST. LOUIS, MISSOURI

Copyright © 2007 by Janice Haywood

All rights reserved. For permission to reuse content, please contact Copyright Clearance Center, 222 Rosewood Drive, Danvers, MA 01923, (978) 750-8400, www.copyright.com.

Scripture quotations, unless otherwise marked, are taken from the HOLY BIBLE, NEW INTERNATIONAL VERSION®. NIV®. Copyright © 1973, 1978, 1984 by International Bible Society. Used by permission of Zondervan Publishing House. All rights reserved.

Cover art: FotoSearch
Cover and interior design: Elizabeth Wright

Visit Chalice Press on the World Wide Web at
www.chalicepress.com

10   9   8   7   6   5   4   3   2   1   07   08   09   10   11   12

Library of Congress Cataloging–in–Publication Data

Haywood, Janice A.
  Enduring connections : creating a preschool and children's ministry / by Janice A. Haywood.
      p. cm.
  Includes bibliographical references and index.
  ISBN-13: 978-0-8272-0821-6 (alk. paper)
  1. Church work with children. I. Title.

  BV639.C4H35 2006
  259'.22--dc22
                                                          2006028827

Printed in the United States of America

Contents

PART 2: Leader of the Ministry

APPENDICES

Introduction

The pastor of a large church once said, "I learned as a pastor that if the preschool ministry was not going well, the rest of the church probably was not going well either." After many years of ministry in a variety of churches, this observant pastor had identified one often-reliable barometer of church health.

Why would preschool and grade-school ministry be such an indicator of the state of a church? (For the purpose of this book, the term "preschoolers" refers to persons from birth until they enter first grade. "Grade-schoolers" refer to persons in grades 1–6 or 6–11 years of age.) My personal assessment is that childhood ministry touches families in profound ways. When a caring church values and nurtures children, church members also encourage and nurture the faith of all of the family members.

Preschool and grade-school ministry is very labor-intensive, requiring a large number of committed volunteer leaders to meet the physical, emotional, and faith needs of their precious children. When a church gives prime attention to ministry to "the least of these," they are more likely to care about other details of ministry as well. The reverse is not predominantly true.

Increasing numbers of ministers and laypersons are recognizing the importance of their childhood ministry to the health of their church.

- Parents value their children. Not only do they want the "very best" for their children, but they seek assistance and encouragement in their parental role.
- Ministers recognize that an effective, safe childhood ministry attracts young families.
- Churches understand that faith is built most effectively from childhood, and strong churches can help build strong spiritual foundations.
- Insightful parents, ministers, and church leadership acknowledge that if the church is to impact our pagan world with the hopeful gospel message, we must begin with children.

Childhood Ministry Makes a Difference in the Lives of Children

Several prominent researchers[1] have documented that the majority of people make their lifelong, faith-shaping choices and form their values when they are young. In a world competing in creative ways for the attention of our children, churches must offer meaningful, stimulating, age-appropriate learning and worship experiences. They also need teachers who will reveal the nature of God within their relationships with the children.

People's attitudes toward church and God are often well formed by the time they reach early adulthood or even their teen years. Children respond to an attractive and safe space for learning and worshiping. They eagerly anticipate the special time spent with their caring and committed teachers at church. A child's enthusiasm can motivate even the reluctant or weary parent who is thinking about "skipping church" that day.

Quality church experiences become especially critical for the child whose parents do not attend church or practice faith in the home. The church that reaches out to these children and their parents finds a mission field "ripe for harvest" (Jn. 4:35b). If most faith decisions are made when people are young, then the vital church must give serious attention and resources to ministry with children from birth.

Childhood Ministry Makes a Difference for Families

Many well-meaning churches have assumed the primary faith-teaching responsibility of parents, and many caring parents have relinquished their faith-nurturing role to the church. Today's families come in all shapes and sizes. All of these families need support, encouragement, and assistance in their God-given responsibility to "impress them [God's commandments] on your children" (Deut. 6:7).

Preschool and grade-school ministry involves helping parents to grow in their faith and knowledge of God and providing assistance in how to communicate their faith as they nurture their children. The church needs to plan intentionally how it will supplement the parents' home instruction when the children are in church.

The congregation that gives serious effort to reaching children whose parents are not involved in church also must give equal ministry effort to reaching those parents. Offering "a cup of water" is good, but "providing the well" is better for nurturing a child's growing faith. Parents who live their faith will have a greater impact on a child than a church experience alone can provide.

Childhood Ministry Makes a Difference to the Church

In today's world, most parents are looking for quality experiences for their children in school, sports, and music, as well as church. Children likewise have come to expect innovative, stimulating learning experiences in all of their activities.

The church that desires to reach young adult couples must have a first-class preschool and grade-school ministry. Adequate and attractive space, quality programming, family-friendly worship, as well as a safe and secure environment are elements that are of the highest consideration for parents who are selecting a church. Today's parents are looking for a church in which their children will be happy with teachers who truly care about the children and are prepared to have meaningful, appropriate learning experiences with them. After they find a church that meets that criterion, then they consider the other aspects of a church's ministry.

One youth and children's minister explained that she had asked for the children's ministry to be added to her youth job description several years earlier. As the children's ministry under her leadership became more intentional in its teaching and discipling, and as the children later became youth, they were ready for a deeper faith experience than the youth in the past were. A church that gives serious attention to the faith formation of all ages might discover that it has more spiritually mature members in the future.[2]

Childhood Ministry Makes a Difference to the Kingdom

Faith formation in the Old Testament Hebrew nation rested primarily on the parents (Deut. 6:6–9), but the Jewish community was an extension of the family. God instructed parents to teach the children the commandments and to include the children in all of their faith practices. This preparation insured the development of individual faith as well as the spiritual strength of the Jewish nation.

Jesus taught us in Matthew 18:3–4 that "unless you change and become like little children, you will never enter the kingdom of heaven." Jesus went on to explain to his disciples that "whoever humbles himself like this child is the greatest in the kingdom of heaven." Not only do children need us to teach them and model a Christ-following lifestyle, but also we need them to remind us of what our relationship with our heavenly parent is at its essence.

When we read Jesus' blessing of the children in Matthew 19:13–15, we often envision a kindly Jesus taking a break from his busy schedule to enjoy the children. The Jewish blessing was very a powerful ritual that was more than a pat on the head. When Jesus placed his hands on the children and blessed them, he was initiating in them a force that would forever empower their lives. Jesus was asking for God, on the behalf of the children, to bring good into their lives. Because the parents had such respect for this great teacher, they believed that a blessing from him would carry great meaning because of his obvious relationship with God.

We, too, can bless the children through our words and through our relationships, but we have to understand the influence that we have. As we bless children in our families and in our church ministries, we set in motion a power in their lives that will connect them to God and to other believers. In Mark 9:36–37, Jesus teaches his disciples (and us) a very valuable lesson about God.

> He took a little child and had him stand among them. Taking him in his arms, he said to them, "Whoever welcomes one of these

little children in my name welcomes me; and whoever welcomes me does not welcome me but the one who sent me."

What does "welcoming children" mean? When we are teaching children or including children as an important ministry, we are in the very presence of God. When children are welcomed into our midst, God is in our midst. When children are excluded from church activities or are given less than the best teachers, facilities, and instruction, we are shortchanging God.

A church can provide a multitude of activities without developing Christ followers. Preschool and grade-school ministry must be more than childcare, entertainment, and/or activities. It must be more than providing "childcare" while parents are engaged in learning or worshiping. Church staff, parents, and lay leadership must know what preschoolers and grade-schoolers need to learn at each stage of development so that a curriculum can be designed to provide a strong foundation for Christian conversion and discipleship. Every time children are at church they need to be taught from the goals and expectations set by the parents and church for the nurturing of their children.

Myths about Effective Childhood Ministry

The success of any ministry is often evaluated by many different criteria. Here are some of the common myths about what makes an effective preschool and grade-school ministry:

Myth 1:"If such large numbers of children are coming to (activity), then it must be effective."

Some people measure success by the *number of people* who participate. If large numbers of children are involved in a ministry, then they judge it as successful without measuring the results of the involvement. However, some adults who attended church as children know very little about the Bible or the application of biblical truths to their lives. The church they attended knew how to draw children, but did not know how to disciple them. Children will respond to many activities at church, especially if their friends attend, regardless of the content received.

Myth 2:"If this church has a large, wide variety of programming for children, then it must be effective."

Parents often look for a wide *variety* of events or activities. They want music, missions education/action, Bible memory, Bible study, camps, fellowship activities, discipleship instruction, sports activities, weekday preschool programs, after-school childcare, etc. As a result, some churches think that they must provide every program, ministry, or activity parents and children desire. In reality, very few churches have the resources to provide a wide array of ministries while maintaining the quality and integrity of the content of the programs they already provide.

Myth 3: "If children are having fun, then it must be effective."

Some people look for churches with innovative, entertaining, or "fun" events. Children will respond to fun activities at church, especially if their friends attend, regardless of the intrinsic value of the content received. I call them "empty calories." Most children would choose a diet of their favorite junk food, but we have an obligation to provide a balanced diet with good nutrients that will contribute to a healthy development. Likewise, all fun is not learning, but all learning can be fun when balanced between good content and engaging teaching methodology. Churches often use cute gimmicks to attract children and their families to the church because they can get immediate results; but after the families are in church, no substantial spiritual nourishment is provided.

Myth 4: "If there are many opportunities for my child to be at church, then it must be effective."

Some parents count the *number* of events or activities provided for preschoolers or grade-schoolers. They want events happening at the church several times a week, especially for the grade-school child. They believe that children's schedules need to be heavily programmed much like those of teenagers, and what better place to have children "dropped off" than at church! This is often true of families who home school and depend on the church for the socialization aspects of their children's development. However, churches that rely on volunteer (often parent) leadership for the most part will find that providing a rigorous schedule of activities for children will "burn out" the leadership core as well as the children. Again, the quality of the program offerings suffer.

Myth 5: "If this church teaches (specified content), then it is effective."

People often evaluate the *content* of the programs based on their pet content. They want programs that have certain content, regardless of how effectively it is taught or how many children are involved. They are looking for specific content such as Bible memorization, biblical content, rote memorization of Scripture and/or doctrine, or other content that meets their standard of excellence without consideration of appropriate educational or life application needs of children and without consideration of a balanced, comprehensive content. Content is important, but the way the content is taught or presented affects whether the children engage the content and integrate it into their lives for more than an hour or two.

A Better Ministry Strategy

While all of these measures have some importance, other criteria may indicate the depth and strength of a church's ministry to preschoolers, grade-schoolers, and their families. As I have ministered in seven churches and consulted with hundreds of churches and ministers in the past thirty-three years, I have identified some of the measures of successful preschool and grade-school ministries in a variety of churches. The church personalities, styles, and sizes are diverse; but the core values are quite similar in the congregations that successfully connect children to God, children and parents to a community of faith, and childhood ministry to the mission and/or vision of the congregation.

These churches are interested in more than activities and numbers. They want to make a significant difference in the spiritual lives of children, families, and the church; so, they have moved beyond both mediocre pro......gramming and "edutainment" fads to embrace a ministry strategy that is both foundational and inviting to children and families. They have ministered to children who have grown into youth and adults as faithful Christ-followers. They have attracted, encouraged, and equipped families to be the faith nurturers of all of the family members. They have grown churches that embrace all members from the youngest to the oldest, and they have thrived.

Many churches are discovering that childhood ministry is deeply rooted in relationships. They are committed to proclaiming Bible truths and stories with integrity rather than simply providing programming that has a biblical theme. They recognize that childhood ministry is first and foremost family ministry. They have found ways to be inclusive of children in their congregational experiences rather than always providing a separate event just for the children. They recognize that "family ministry" is not just providing activities for all ages of family members, but it includes providing experiences in which the whole family can participate together.

This book is written especially for the minister or layperson who guides the childhood ministry in a church—a person who passionately believes in building "Enduring Connections" between a child and God, and a child and a faith community. Those "Enduring Connections" are rooted in relationships with parents, teachers, ministers, and others who care deeply for the children and live and speak of their faith.

Each chapter poses a question that will guide you in evaluating or beginning such a childhood ministry that weaves *Enduring Connections*.

Notes

[1] George Barna, *Transforming Children into Spiritual Champions* (Ventura, Calif.: Issachar Resources, 2003), 43; and Thom S. Rainer, *The Bridger Generation* (Nashville: Broadman & Holman), 1997, ix.

[2] Ibid., 65.

PART 1: THE CHILDHOOD MINISTRY

Does Your Church Have a Focused Goal or Vision for Preschool and Grade-school Ministry?

Every church needs to answer these questions:

- What do we want preschoolers to know about God and experience before they enter first grade? How can we best help them to accomplish that?
- What do we want grade-schoolers to know about God and experience before they enter seventh grade? How can we best help them to accomplish that?
- What will our role be in encouraging and equipping families?

A congregation's answers to these questions will guide the structure, programming, scheduling, and content of its ministry. When a church knows what it wants to accomplish, it has direction for getting there.

This is "easier said than done." The majority of churches have only a vague notion of what they are trying to accomplish with their children and families. At worst, some congregations have "time slots" that they fill with a variety of activities that are appealing to children and parents. However, the programs often are not connected with each other in any way even though they are ministering to the same group of children. Teachers seldom are aware of the content of other ministries, and sometimes they are rotating in and out of classes, even unaware of what was taught or experienced in the previous session of the same ministry.

Many churches simply repeat the programs that they have traditionally provided, only tweaking or updating them slightly from year to year. Other churches look to a "booming" church in their community or even another city and attempt to repeat the programs that church is doing in an effort to replicate the perceived success. They have not given serious consideration to evaluating whether they are effectively laying strong faith foundations with children in their church because most of them have not discussed nor determined what that would "look like."

Instead of scheduling a series of activities, programs, or ministries with preschoolers and grade-schoolers, what if a church began envisioning how they could help preschoolers, grade-schoolers, and their families to become all God wants them to be? What if they were intentional in planning a "curriculum" that addressed all of the aspects of spiritual formation, especially the foundational portion of the preschool years and the grade school years?

God's Vision

In Matthew 22:37–40 Jesus told us what God desires from all people. Put simply, we are to love God and love others. The question that every congregation needs to ask is: What is being done to help children to love God with all their hearts, souls, and minds? Is the ministry focused on God? Does it help the children to love God more? Is the ministry outwardly focused, encouraging children to love others—all kinds of "others"?

If you start with God's vision of how to live out that great commandment in *your* church and *your* community, your ministry vision will be unique. The people, resources, gifts, and even the context of your church will make God's vision for your church different from that of any other church. Instead of simply adopting what another church may be doing and then asking God to bless it, consider asking God what his vision is for your church and letting him guide your journey.

This discovery of God's vision begins with prayer—a lot of prayer, not just a "bless us" before the meeting starts and at the end. Begin by imagining what God could do in your childhood ministry. Don't be afraid to dream God-sized dreams. By seeking first "his kingdom" rather than your own, you will find that God will be able to guide you to his future.

The discovery also may mean visiting other churches that seem to be thriving through living out God's vision for their church. "Priming your vision pump" through these visits needs to be followed by evaluating what "learnings" God might be guiding you toward. Explore how you might adapt rather than adopt elements of what other churches are doing that seem applicable to what you want to accomplish in your ministry.

Talking It Out and Putting It Down

Depending on the organizational structure and church polity, each congregation needs to involve the people most affected by the ministry. One suggested grouping could be a Childhood Ministry Team (see chapter 12). This team of key preschool and grade-school leadership and representative parents would begin the process of determining the vision for the church's ministry to preschoolers, grade-schoolers, and their families by considering several things:

1. Assess what your church is doing very well. If you are fortunate, you have some leadership with passions in certain areas of childhood ministry. People with passion give much time and energy to sharing that passion with children and other leadership. However, you need to be realistic about how well the current ministries are being implemented. Are some age groups doing well while others are struggling? Are some existing programs energized while others are "tired?" Get input from parents and leaders as well as children. Assessment can be done through interviews or surveys (see appendix 1).

Build on your strengths. Many times churches begin by attempting to strengthen their weaknesses first. Congregations have a limited amount of resources, and if they funnel their energies to weakest areas, the strong areas often begin struggling. A wiser course is to make the strong programs that support your vision and your goals even more effective and appealing. As people are energized by the results of these efforts and additional leadership emerges, the weaker areas can be addressed. Sometimes the ineffective programs need to cease, and sometimes they can be reinvented or revitalized.

2. Look at the church's vision statement (if there is one) and discuss how the preschool and grade-school ministry helps to accomplish what the church has identified as its unique role in the world. If your church does not have a vision statement, then seek God's vision for the preschool and grade-school ministry. What hope or support could your church offer to children and families in your community, town, or city? Look within the family needs in the congregation, but also look outside the congregation. What ministry needs in your community are you uniquely equipped to meet? Here are examples of vision statements:

- To encourage, equip, and empower parents and leadership to be purposeful in the Christlike development of children (see Lk. 2:52).
- To assist and guide children in all areas of development so that they will come to know Christ and have a personal relationship with him.
- To integrate childhood ministry into every aspect of the church's ministry: education, missions, worship, fellowship, and evangelism.

The vision statement will give the guiding team its overall direction and basis for selecting and implementing programs, as well as for eliminating existing programs that do not support the vision.

3. Guided by the vision, the team also will be ready to develop a list of what they want preschoolers and grade-schoolers to know and experience before they move to the next age grouping. This process will take

considerable discussion, negotiation, and—eventually—consensus. Initially consider broad concepts, skills, or experiences rather than a detailed listing of Bible content, skills, activities, etc. For example, the team may list valued concepts and experiences:

- Bible skills appropriate for each age level
- Inquirer's classes for third through sixth graders
- Worship orientation sessions before 4-year-olds attend congregational worship services (or whatever age begins congregational worship)
- Outreach activities for unchurched children
- Mission education and/or mission action activities for children
- Intergenerational Bible study experiences

Next, the team may compose a list of Bible concepts and Bible skills that will be taught at each age as they consider the developmental needs of preschoolers and grade-schoolers. Some churches weave those concepts throughout all of their ministries to that age group. Appendix 2 has a sample portion of one church's document that guides the teaching of their preschoolers and grade-schoolers.

4. Next consider how to equip leaders/teachers and parents to accomplish the vision. This will involve another listing based on the vision. For example, a team might plan the following:

- Parent education workshops/seminars four times a year
- Family Bible study classes for all ages once a quarter
- Age group leadership training once a month
- Outreach activities for unchurched families

After the list is made, the team would do well to prioritize the equipping activities since most churches tend to list more than they can realistically execute with excellence.

5. Before adding further detail to the annual plan, take the vision and the broad listing of the plan implementation to a larger audience to involve more people in "owning" and supporting the ministry. Again, depending on the church's organization and operating procedures, the report might be presented to a church coordinating team or to all parents and leadership. Make sure that the plan has the support and input of the church staff, especially the pastor in most churches, before presenting it to the larger group.

If you encounter resistance, consider the validity of the opposition and either take the time to discuss the issues until the opposition is dispersed or redo the plan before proceeding.

6. Once you have reported to the larger group(s), made adjustments based on any input, and secured official approval (if needed) to proceed, you are ready to make annual plans.

Annual Planning

Many churches seem to plan from one activity to another, but a yearly plan will move you from an activity-based to a vision-guided ministry. Armed with your vision, the listing of what you want the children to know and experience in your church, and the leadership/parent training events needed, the team is ready to determine the yearly plan. Not only will you determine the activities to accomplish your vision, but also you will calendar them, prepare a budget, and secure resources needed to accomplish them. Some churches choose a theme or a focus for their yearly programs, activities, and emphases chosen from the identified priorities in the visioning phase. For example, you may champion a family emphasis that will feature activities or programs that include the whole family in some way. Not every program will be multigenerational, but there may be elements of how to involve the family in the child's learning experience.

For example, one church chose a family emphasis several years ago. They planned a family activity for each quarter. At Christmas, families constructed a tabletop family nativity built from pre-cut stable kits and a variety of materials for the figures. The church even created a family vacation Bible school that was multigenerational rather than age-graded. They planned ways to communicate what the preschoolers and grade-schoolers were learning in their Bible study, missions, and music programs throughout the year. They made suggestions for how the learning could be expanded at home during the week. They sought ways to make the worship services more family inclusive, with children participating as worship leaders from time to time.

Regularly occurring ministries such as weekly Bible study, music/choir programs, or discipleship ministries will need adequate planning and support. Coordination of these ministries will be essential for them to be complementary to each other. Basically the same children will be involved in all of the programs, so rather than being competitive, each ministry needs to have a unique role in what the church wants to accomplish in the life of the child. Of course, some repetition will remain, but that should be planned to reinforce the concepts and experiences. The plan must give each ministry a unique contribution to the faith formation of the preschoolers and grade-schoolers without being simply redundant.

The ongoing programs will be the heart of the church's ministry, so give adequate attention to the actions necessary for implementation. Work out the details of:

- *Scheduling*–Determine weekly or monthly regularly scheduled time (including the duration of each session), launch date, and ending date (if applicable). Discuss any necessary variation from the weekly/monthly schedule for interruptions due to holidays, summer, or other break.

- *Leadership*–Follow the procedures of your church for identifying and securing adequate, competent leadership. If you cannot discover the kind of leadership needed to provide an effective ministry, delay the launch until you can enlist leadership, or reorganize the groupings until additional leadership can be secured.
- *Space*–Often multiple programs use the same rooms. Determine which rooms scheduled programs will use. Facilitate the cooperative usage of the rooms with the leadership of the various programs. Shared space conflict can be minimized if guidelines are determined from the beginning.
- *Literature*–Select quality literature for each program/ministry. Find the literature that best matches your vision and values. Preschool and grade-school literature marketing is a prolific business, so know what you want your preschoolers and grade-schoolers to learn, and select the literature that most closely matches your criteria (see chapter 11). The team may want to include some of the leadership in the process.

Next, the team will set the dates for the activities/events they have selected that are not regularly scheduled programs. Be sure to check the church as well as community calendars to avoid creating obvious conflicts. It is easy to feel that the planning is done when a date is on the calendar, but the preparation phase is only the beginning. Determine what needs to be done to make it happen, and write down those actions for the team that will eventually carry out the event.

Hopefully, you will be able to submit a budget to the team or group in your church that determines how the church income will be spent. Use your annual plans to itemize the dollar amount that would realistically support the ministry plan. Many childhood ministries do not have the money they need to have excellent programs because they have not captured a God-sized vision that is clearly communicated to the church. This is your opportunity to communicate your vision as well as what it would take to provide this excellent, visionary ministry. Sharing your vision, your plans, and especially the benefit to the church itself will more likely secure the funds needed for implementation. If you receive less money than requested or needed, adjust your plans based on your priorities.

Once the plans and the budget are finalized, implement the rest of the plan as outlined in chapter 12. Periodically, the planning team needs to evaluate the effectiveness of the annual plan and make necessary adjustments or additions.

CHAPTER 2

Does Your Church Consider Children a Valued Component of the Congregation?

Churches take one of two predominate approaches to childhood ministry. One approach desires "care" for preschoolers and grade-schoolers so that the important aspects of church can take place. In other words, the church views children's ministry as a support ministry of the church. Some churches want it done with quality, and others give it little thought or attention as long as nothing unfortunate happens. The guiding principle for these churches is that preschool and grade-school ministry is important only as it satisfies parents and enables them to participate in the "real" ministries of the church while the children are "provided for."

Churches with this "childcare" perspective will give minimum effort and resources until a crisis arises or people complain. Parents, leadership, or sometimes even childhood ministers or directors who expect more than "care" often are viewed as troublemakers or "whiners." The leadership must constantly appeal for financial resources, desirable space, quality leadership, and even church staff assigned to minister to the children and their leadership. Preschool and grade-school ministry is seldom visible to the church at large and is rarely mentioned from the pulpit unless "workers" are needed.

However, an increasing number of churches are recognizing childhood ministry as a key ministry of the church. It is considered vital to a vibrant church and the growing faith of its preschoolers and grade-schoolers.

Assessing Value

Several indicators reveal whether a church values preschool and grade-school ministry as a part of its overall mission.

1. Evaluate the space designated for preschool and grade-school children— location, attractiveness, spaciousness, and furnishings as well as safety.

Compare the children's space to the adult classrooms and the youth area. Children do not have the power or ability to demand better space, but they often *feel* that their space is not inviting. Children may express their displeasure by not wanting to go to "their room." The first impression visiting families have of a church is the appearance of the space where they are expected to leave their preschoolers or grade-schoolers. Many people do not return because of the impression that this church does not value children by designating quality space and furnishings for teaching and ministry events. In addition, the protection of children is increasingly important, and parents are looking for security measures that insure the safety of their children. (See chapter 10 for an expansion on this value indicator.)

2. Observe the congregation's treatment of children.

I have a personal practice of greeting children before I greet their parents. I once had a mother tell me months after they had started to attend the church in which I worked that she was offended the first time I greeted her child first because she had never had that to happen before. She confessed that once she understood how much it meant to her child, she was grateful for a church that valued her child that much.

Adults that value children do not look over children or through children, but they greet the children as well as their parents. A child that is greeted with eye contact on his or her level feels important and accepted. Congregations that value children have drinking fountains on the child's level and lower visual interest in hallways. Some churches even provide booster chairs for the pews or seats in the sanctuary or auditorium.

Preschoolers and grade-schoolers need to receive the same contact from the church that their parents do. For example, if e-mails or cards are sent to adults, children should receive them as well, especially from their ministry leadership. If adults receive a box of offering envelopes, the children should, too. If adults receive ministry visits as a result of a death or another crisis occurrence, then the children are visited, too. Children may not have the same knowledge that adults do, but they have the same emotions. They and their parents can sense whether the children are considered important or not by the way you treat them.

3. Examine the budget.

Compare the number of preschoolers and grade-schoolers to the amount of the budget line items for their ministry. Some of the designated funds may be included in general "literature," "education," or "supplies" line items, but you can get a rough figure for budgeted expenditures per child. Do a similar comparison for youth and adult ministries. I am not suggesting that the amounts should be equal, but they should not be hugely disproportionate either. Consider including salaries of age group or education ministers assigned to the various ministry areas. Churches almost always put their resources into the ministries they value most—buildings, certain people groups, missions/outreach, staff, etc. What does the church budget suggest that your church values most?

4. Consider church activities.

When events are planned, is consideration given to how to include children in the purpose of the event or activity? Perhaps the church automatically considers "childcare" since they do not consider how children might be able to experience the purpose of the activity. At the least, does the church even think of providing childcare as a part of the planning process rather than as an afterthought?

For example, if the church is planning a special Wednesday evening Thanksgiving service, does it

a. consider how to plan a multigenerational service that is inclusive of children (as well as other age groups) as active participants?
b. provide a children's event that leads them in a time of thankfulness?
c. separate the children and "pop in" a cartoon video (or another accept-able, low-preparation activity)?

While the first option is preferable, the second would be better than the third. Children need to learn how to be thankful and express thankfulness to God, not just learn about the pilgrims (who are not biblical) or a cartoon character (who is not even a real person!).

A church that considers children important to its mission will take advantage of any time it has children at church. Consider what a church is providing for preschoolers and grade-schoolers during adult choir practice, during worship services, or during small group Bible studies in homes. Often this time is simply "babysitting," but it could be a teaching time if literature, leadership, and materials were encouraged and furnished.

5. Determine whether there is a staff minister who gives priority time to this ministry.

It may not be his or her sole ministry responsibility, but is there an assigned staff minister who is advocating and equipping the leadership to perform an excellent childhood ministry?

Sometimes a church will "hire" a layperson to "direct" the work, but the church may not value the ministry enough to call him or her a minister or include that person in staff meetings or as a worship leader. Sometimes they call him or her a "minister," but the church does not encourage "the minister" to get the training needed to be effective in the assigned ministry. In other words, the "director" or "coordinator" has low visibility, and the church has low expectations. A church with this pattern will "burn through" many leaders in a short time.

A church that values children will empower and support someone to give preschool and grade-school ministry a "fair share" of her or his time and commitment, whether the person receives a salary or is a volunteer. Increasing numbers of churches are recognizing the value of a part-time or full-time paid staff minister. Many congregations elect involved, committed laypersons to assume official leadership of childhood ministry. Those who are "called out" from the lay leadership often have the passion and commitment but not the information and training to guide an excellent ministry. In those cases, many churches are investing in certification programs or educational experiences to equip those who are called and committed to preschool and/or grade-school children's ministry in that congregation.

6. Gauge the support of preschool and grade-school ministry by the senior pastor.

When a senior pastor gives public support of a ministry, whether it is from the pulpit or at other times, the importance of the ministry is elevated. Recognizing the successes of the ministry and encouraging involvement in the ministry indicate that the senior pastor truly values the children and the leadership.

Private recognition, affirmation, and encouragement of the preschoolers, grade-schoolers, and the leaders also denote the value the pastor places on this age group ministry. Is the senior pastor seen in the preschool and grade-school hallway once in a while? Does the senior pastor know and acknowledge the children by name? Does the senior pastor invite the age group minister to have leadership responsibilities in worship?

7. Assess worship involvement.

One important indicator of a church's commitment to ministry with preschoolers and grade-schoolers is the area of worship. Since often the first church event a guest will attend is a worship service, inclusion of children in the worship experience is a strong indicator to parents who are looking for an effective ministry for their children. However, some parents consider an effective worship ministry for their children to be a separate children's worship service.

In a church that views children as a valued part of the congregation, the worship needs of children and families are valued as much as the worship needs of adults and youth. Churches have become so effective with age-graded activities that in some churches age groups rarely mix anymore. Children are with children and their age-group leadership whenever they are at church. Churches have become age-group friendly rather than family-friendly. Worship is one time a church can minister to families as a whole.

While some parents and churches may consider a "children's church service" as an indicator that children are valued, a church that is willing to be inclusive of children in the congregational worship service may value children even more because they intentionally plan for a worship experience that is inviting to all ages. "Children's church" in many churches is an effort to provide something for the children so the parents do not have to "deal with" their children; and, more often than not, it does not have consistent leadership committed to quality worship.

Worship and Children

Every church must be intentional in providing the best possible worship experiences for all ages, including children. We were created to worship Almighty God, and that begins with infancy. Psalm 8:2 tells us, "From the lips of children and infants / you have ordained praise." That verse is very clear that since God is the recipient in worship, children can worship God, too. It isn't about cognition but about an attitude of "telling God how much we love him." How your church meets the worship needs and interests of your children and the congregation must be considered, discussed, and decided thoughtfully and prayerfully.

What are the benefits for children being in a "family" worship service?

- Children see their parents and other adults and youth engage in the significant worship of Almighty God. Parental modeling and conversation are the most powerful influencers in faith development.[1] A worship service may be the only time that children see their parents engage in worship. With the hectic schedule of today's families, many children never observe their parents in worship at home. They may or may not have nighttime prayers or blessings at meals, *when* the family does find time to eat together. Stressed parents often use the early morning or late night quiet to do their personal devotions, a practice children do not observe.
- Children need to feel the "welcoming" of the church at large–they need to feel that they are part of something bigger than their own age group ministry. Children who are never with "the whole church" may not sense that they are a part of a church "family" that has faith grandparents, aunts, uncles, and cousins, as well as brothers and sisters.
- Children need to hear the testimonies of mature Christians. Prayer, Word, music, or another worship expression reveals the personal faith journey of growing Christians and communicates hope even to children. They may not understand all of the meaning, but they do sense the importance of the testimony and of the working of God in the lives of others.
- A congregation needs to be reminded of the future. The presence of children keeps a church from becoming self-absorbed in meeting only immediate needs. A balanced congregation needs the presence of the past (senior adults), the present (parents and other adults), and the future (preschoolers and grade-schoolers).[2] When children are not present, adults may miss the fresh perspective that children often add to a worship practice long taken for granted. Observing children as

worship leaders reminds adults that church is not all about "me," but about "us" and our collective relationship with the Living God.
- Children need to experience the church in all of its expressions–baptism, communion, deacon/elder ordination, parent-child dedications, mission trip commissioning, etc. They will raise many questions. Adults will find no simple answers to many of these "children's questions," but they will perceive the importance of the moment. Children who are not present in "big church" may not experience these special "family times" full of meaning and emotion.

What about parents?

Parents bear most of the responsibility for guiding children in worship, and yet parents are often the most resistant to children, especially younger grade-school children, being with them in worship. Their primary reasons are that the children are not "getting anything out of it" or that the activity of their children so distracts the parents that *they* are not "getting anything out of it."

Because parents have an enormous responsibility and because this is such an important time for the formation of their child's faith, they need to consider two things:

1. Most aspects of worship/faith are not taught–they are experienced and modeled by people significant in the life of the child. Just because children may not be "sitting still and listening," we cannot assume that they are not paying attention. Parents or churches can provide activities to keep children's wiggling to a minimum. In doing so, both church and parents need to be aware that today's children, especially grade-school children, often multitask. They watch television *and* do homework. They play games on the computer *and* watch television. They read *and* hear the conversation between parents. They wiggle and work in an activity booklet, *and still* are participants in an experience of worship. For them worship involves more than listening–it includes all of their senses. You can be sure that they are benefiting from being with your family as well as "the family of God" even though they may tell their parents otherwise. Particularly grade-schoolers will speak negatively of going to school and church, as well as other places that are not particularly entertaining. Parents are still guiding children as they grow, and some things are just "good for them" whether the children would choose them or not if given a preference. Instead of being judgmental of parents who may have an unusually active child, caring adults in the congregation can offer to let the child sit with them occasionally. Children often behave better for people other than their own parents. This may give the child much-needed spiritual aunts or grandfathers.

2. You have a "window of opportunity" in children's development during which they are especially sensitive to what their parents think and believe. Many times parents must sacrifice their own desires to meet the

needs of their children, and this is one of those times. As parents involve and encourage their child in worship, the child will begin to connect emotionally to a powerful corporate experience. Many churches are experiencing children who grow up in "children's church," have no emotional connection to the larger family, and thus choose not to attend as teens because it is "not for them."

How can worship leaders include children in the worship experience?

Worship leaders must consider how they can be inclusive of children and families in the worship experience. A church that expects children to sit still while adults worship is not being sensitive to the needs of the whole church family. Here are a few ways worship leaders have included children in family-friendly churches:

- Provide children's worship guides. You may create guides related to the service or purchase guides from a preprinted children's bulletin service. The former is more effective but labor intensive and requires advanced cooperation of the worship leadership. The copied bulletin from a supplier may not always relate directly to the elements of the worship service they are attending, but the children are occupied while their senses take in the worship experience.
- Let children hand out worship guides (bulletins) at the door, a task they enjoy.
- Let children greet worshipers as they enter the worship center, particularly other children.
- Let children gather the offering.
- Encourage children to contribute to the offering as an act of worship.
- Include a special time for communicating with the children through children's sermons or, even better, by directing a few minutes of the main sermon toward the children, who respond especially to stories—biblical and personal.
- Enlist children as worship leaders to lead in a responsive reading or litany, to pray, or to read Scripture, according to their abilities and interests.
- Invite children to play an instrument or sing (not necessarily as a children's choir), teaching them to direct their musical worship to God instead of performing for adults.
- Convey the message to children worship leaders that they are helping the adults to worship, too.
- Make children responsible for a special ritual for signaling the start of each service—lighting candles or opening a Bible or kneeling at the altar in silent prayer, for example.
- Encourage grade-schoolers to write litanies, prayers, or poems and then use their thoughts in the worship service.

- Call on children to assist in parent/child dedication ceremonies by presenting the certificate or gift. In some faith traditions they can participate in infant baptisms.
- Provide assistance for parents in how they can guide their child in worship (see appendix 3).
- Encourage the congregation to be supportive of parents and their children as they learn how to be participants in worship.

How can a church help preschoolers worship?

While older preschoolers may attend a short service or part of a worship service, the church may need to provide worship experiences on their level of activity and understanding. Before kindergarten, preschoolers do not need a structured worship experience (children's "church"), but rather they need planned activities through which they worship in their spontaneous way. It should not be a "play" time or a "childcare" time, but rather a teaching/worshiping time with teachers who guide the preschoolers' thoughts as they are busy with planned learning/worship activities.

What about a children's worship service?

When a church considers starting a children's worship service, they first need to determine why they want to start a separate service. Their answer to this question will affect the children and the ministry profoundly. They will probably discover a mixture of motives. Above all, a church must want to provide the best possible worship experiences for children and not just want to get them out of the adults' way. Here are some of the reasons a church might provide a separate children's worship service:

- A number of children attend church without parents to guide them although some churches encourage families to "adopt a child" for the purpose of guiding him or her in a worship experience.
- Many "seeker" parents need to hear the gospel. Some seeker parents are too distracted by their children, but increasing numbers are indicating that they want their children with them, especially if the service is geared to all ages.
- Worship leaders and/or the congregation are unwilling to be inclusive of children in the congregational worship service. Children sense when they are not welcome.
- The church wants to prepare children for worship through a short-term worship education process. For several weeks, preschoolers transitioning into the worship service are instructed in the elements of a worship experience as well as the meaning behind them. Church conduct as well as how they can contribute to the worship experience are emphasized.
- Parents are unwilling to accept their God-given responsibility. While the church is "growing" them to assume that responsibility, the church

may need to offer a short-term "interim" service for the grade-school children.

If a church decides to provide a separate worship service for grade-school children, it needs to carefully consider these suggestions:

- Let the children participate in the congregational worship experience for part of the service. This may be the only time they will see parents worship, a powerful role model during this age of faith formation. It also gives them an opportunity to know the worship leaders. If they are never in the congregational worship experience, they may never experience the ministry of the worship leaders. That may be especially detrimental when it is time for them to make a public profession of faith.
- Provide a true worship experience, not videos, playtime, or entertainment. Select leadership who will develop meaningful relationships with the children. This will take planning and commitment on the part of leadership. Build this ministry on the assumption that this is not a convenience for parents but a ministry for children.
- Insist that children "graduate" from the children's worship experience no later than the fourth grade, and earlier if possible.
- Provide consistent adult leadership. Just as churches do not like to have rotating pastors preaching each Sunday, children have an even harder time with rotating leadership. Children need consistency in discipline, teaching, and relationship. Keep the rotation as infrequent and with as few people as possible. In addition, maintain a one adult for every six children ratio (1/6) with never fewer than two unrelated adults with any group of children.

Our real core values are those that we live rather than those we say we believe. A church may say they value children, but the proof is demonstrated by where they are allocating their money, time, and energy.

Notes

[1] Peter L. Benson and Carolyn H. Elkin, *Effective Christian Education: A national study of Protestant congregations—a summary report on faith, loyalty, and congregational life* (Minneapolis: Search Institute, 1990). This study found that the top two influencers of a person's faith maturity were conversations with mother and father.

[2] John H. Westerhoff III, *Will Our Children Have Faith?* rev. ed. (Harrisburg, Pa.: Morehouse Publishing, 2000).

CHAPTER 3

Do Parents Receive Support, Encouragement, and Resources from the Church?

Never an easy task, parenting is still rewarding but more challenging than ever. Our ever-expanding communications network brings the world and all of its negative as well as positive influences into the lives of children. Many children of past generations had limited exposure to anything outside of their community, but with the increasing influence of television[1] and the Internet, coupled with shrinking parental (or adult) supervision, children are bombarded with images and concepts from a variety of value systems and beliefs. Children are the target of a billion dollar marketing strategy that includes everything from designer clothing for children to high-tech toys and vacation destinations. Children exercise more and more influence on how families spend their resources.

The more the church can help to inform, support, and/or educate parents, the more it helps children and families in general. Many of the powerful cultural influences on children also powerfully influence parents, who may or may not be aware of the impact on them or their children. The American society is consumer driven. Thus our families can become driven consumers if parents do not critically evaluate the seductive messages often contradicting their Christian values. Parents who seriously assess the messages of commercials, monitor children's computer usage, and evaluate life's daily messages in light of their value system can powerfully impact the critical thinking ability of their children and assist them in eventually making their own ethical decisions based on Christian values rather than cultural values.

Parents want the best for their children, but in our consumer-driven society, they have learned to secure the services of others, often "experts," to provide the training, lessons, services that will prepare their children for a successful life. For many parents, the church is another "provider." They expect the church to provide the faith training for their children. However, faith formation of children does not occur solely in a couple of hours a week in a structured setting. Religion can be taught, but faith is a daily weaving of relationship with godly people who exemplify the character of

God until children are developmentally able to relate to God in ways other than through their five senses.

David Elkind fairly presents the necessity for parents to balance the needs of their children with their own needs.[2] Busy parents need to value the impact that they have upon the lives of their children and be willing to prioritize their activities and "be there" when their children are most impressionable.

Parent Faith Needs

Parents themselves often operate from depleted faith resources. It is easy in a world of myriad options to make good choices that are still not the best ones for both parents and their children. If the parents' faith is not prominent in their thoughts and actions, they often miss opportune moments of relating to their children how their faith helps them with their daily challenges. They assume children "see" their lived-out faith, but parents need to interpret or point out the results of faith in their lives to their children who do not have adequate understanding of the meaning of subtle daily expressions or experiences of faith.

To be a "parent of faith," one must find the time to pray, read, and reflect on the meaning of biblical lessons, or to engage in other faith-nurturing activities that draw one into a dynamic relationship with God. As children observe and/or participate in some of these spiritual disciplines, they learn the importance of faith even before they understand the content. Likewise, as parents express how God impacts their lives through routine daily activities, their children see faith at work in their parents' lives.

Churches must encourage parents in their faith journeys. Bible studies, retreats, and other faith-building ministries will help parents to recharge their spiritual lives and thus be better equipped to guide their children in their faith journeys. A church that wants to impact families will have an intentional vision of empowering families to be the "growing place" of faith.

The Problem with Age Grading

Seeking to teach people biblical content that was educationally appropriate for their stage of development, churches during the twentieth century divided people into age groupings. It first started in Sunday school, then expanded into other areas of church programming. Today, very few church activities, particularly in large churches, are multi-aged. The last multi-age experience, worship, is now often age graded: preschoolers in worship care, children in "children's church," and sometimes, even youth in a separate worship service. Some churches have multiple worship services that are attended primarily by certain age groups, thus further age-grading the faith "family."

The positive benefits of age grading, particularly if there is a narrow age span, is that preschoolers and grade-schoolers can be taught biblical concepts and truths as well as life application in ways that relate to them in their current developmental stage. Because the content and application have current meaning to the life of the child, the child is more likely to retain and apply it immediately. Teaching preschoolers and grade-schoolers who are near the same age also is easier for the teacher, who has to do less adapting, although few groups of children are in exactly the same developmental point even though they may be the same chronologically.

Age grading does have shortcomings that are especially detrimental for the family:

- The family is never together when they are at church. Having activities for each member of the family does not mean that a church is "family friendly." Family-friendly churches need to show families how to grow together and assist each other in their faith journey.
- Children have few opportunities to observe the next stage of development that will draw them forward and help them to grow in their faith. Preschoolers watch grade-schoolers, grade-schoolers watch youth, and youth watch adults to get their "cues" for the next passage of development. For example, preschoolers will follow grade-schoolers around, especially older brothers or sisters, much to older siblings' dismay. Grade-schoolers will imitate the clothing and behavior of teens. Teenagers may take up "adult" behaviors to appear mature. In matters of faith, they are observing, too. As they have opportunities to be with people of multiple ages in worship and sometimes in Bible study and fellowship, preschoolers and grade-schoolers begin to hear the faith stories of those older than they are, and parents and other adults benefit from the fresh perspective children can give faith.
- Children do not have an opportunity to see how their parents, teachers, and other significant adults express their faith through worship. With today's hectic family routines, children may not see parents reading the Bible, praying, or singing praises to God except in church. That modeling is crucial.[3] George Barna has found that "less than one out of every twenty churched households ever worships God outside of a church service...or has any type of regular Bible study or devotional time together during a typical week."[4]
- Parents get the impression that the church is responsible for the faith nurturing of their children. Perhaps, the church has unwittingly sent the wrong message: "Bring them to church, and we will provide their spiritual teaching." Now we have parents who do not understand that *they* are the primary faith nurturers of their children. God mandated this in Deuteronomy 6:6–9, and, practically, parents have the most powerful teaching opportunities as they demonstrate loving God and loving others in their daily living.

This does not mean that no activities with preschoolers and grade-school children should ever be age graded. Teaching children on their level of understanding and experience offers many benefits. However, to have a rich faith formation curriculum for the whole family, churches need to consider other possible learning groupings.

Family Faith Experiences

Sometimes a church can form either biological or multigenerational family groupings for the purpose of learning from each other. Young children need to hear how God has been faithful in the lives of their parents and older adults. Adults need to hear about God from a child's perspective, which is often simple and unencumbered with the clutter that can accumulate and distort perceptions throughout a lifetime.

In a plenary session, one church grouped two multiage biological families together and added some senior adults, single adults, or people without their biological families present to each small group formed after the presentation of a Bible story. The members of each small group were instructed to assume the roles of different Bible characters in the story just heard and to process how they might have felt if they had been that person, why they did what they did, and how they could have made another choice. Then each "family grouping" discussed how the story related to their lives. Other family Bible study experiences have involved acting out the story, using art materials to process the story, and writing words about the Bible material for a known melody.

Several churches have come to value this format so much that they have a family Bible study class that meets for three months during the church's Bible study ministry time (often Sunday morning), and they age grade the remaining months. Still others use Christmas, Easter, Thanksgiving, summer, or special times in the church year to have multigenerational events that are Bible study, worship, or fellowship experiences.

Family stories carry a great deal of power as well, and often even members of the family don't know family faith stories.[5] A story night during which parents and children tell other families their stories might be an enlightening experience even within a family. Here is a list of starter questions:

- Tell about a house you have lived in, your favorite room, and why it was/is your favorite.
- When was/is a time that you felt/feel God's presence in your family?
- What was your favorite family vacation?
- What is a family ritual that you have?

As families share their stories, younger children might draw what they are hearing, or older children can write important words they hear on a poster. Any family photos related to the stories could be shared with the story. Some families have started recording the stories in the voice of the family member recounting their faith experiences. Children have stories, impressions, and insights to share as well. One of these family experiences taught a mother how deeply her now teenage child was impacted by a childhood experience that the mother had considered rather insignificant to their family.

Several families have discovered the value of creating a family mission or purpose statement. Through dialogue about what they believe God wants them to contribute as a family to his kingdom, they have created a mission statement that guides the choices they make about how they will spend their time and energy, and even their money. In a world of good choices for both children and parents, the family mission statement helps the family to choose the options that have the most meaning for them and for the difference they want to make in the world.

Other Family Strengthening Experiences

The church can encourage family relationship building through activities that include the whole family. Some churches have tried such events as the following:

- Family scrapbooking with all members of the family contributing
- Family game night with board games or group games
- Family picnics with organized sports played by families rather than by age groups
- Family retreats
- Family mission trips

Survey the families in your church to determine their interests, and tailor the family events to the resources in your community and church.

Parent-equipping Seminars

The community of faith has been very reluctant to provide educational opportunities for parents to improve their parental skills. Aside from occasional sermons, few churches provide seminars, written materials and resources, or support groups so that parents can be more effective teachers and communicators with their children. Most parents feel very inadequate for the task, but often "fly by the seat of their pants" in the absence of assistance in areas such as

- basic child development, allowing parents to be aware of what is considered "normal" developmental behavior, particularly after a preschooler is past the toddler stage
- effective and appropriate discipline techniques to help a child become a self-disciplined, morally ethical adult who follows Jesus' guidelines for behavior
- effective faith formation and counseling for children through the conversion experience

- sex education that reflects Christian values while providing accurate, appropriate information for each stage of development
- death experiences (pets, grandparents, friends)
- divorce recovery for children whose parents have split up
- worship

Part of the dilemma is finding a time to provide seminars parents can or will attend. The church must find suitable times that fit into the schedules of busy, stressed parents. Some churches have found that seminars that fit into the church's regular scheduling work best—Sunday morning, Sunday evening, or whenever the majority of your church members are in attendance. Other churches extend a meeting time for special parenting opportunities, such as early Sunday afternoon, providing a meal and a meaningful activity for the children. Some very intentional congregations calendar weekend family retreats, including family activities and interaction while also providing special seminars for parents and meaningful learning experiences for the children.

Guidance for Communion: A Family or Faith Family Decision

In some denominations, parents dread communion when their church practice or even stated church policy is that nonmembers or children who are not baptized as believers are not invited to take communion. Rather than finding it a time of celebration and meaningful remembrance, they encounter their puzzled children being excluded from a "family ritual." Children who had juice and crackers in their preschool worship care as a snack find it difficult to understand why the adults get juice and crackers and they are passed over.

In churches that do not practice infant baptism, it is important to inform parents of the expectations of the congregation. If it is not stated policy, but commonly held practice, to exclude unbaptized children, then parents need to be informed of the expectations rather than be the object of congregant disapproval when they allow their children to receive the communion elements. Whether they choose to abide by the expectations may be another matter.

A growing number of churches allow parents to make the decision whether to allow their young children to participate in communion. These churches need to provide parent education to guide them in their family discussions and decision-making before the children see the elements offered in the service. One such church provided the following guidelines for parents:

"You may decide to allow your child to participate in communion for some of the following reasons:

- Communion is a family experience, showing inclusion. Participation in communion says to the child: 'You are a valued part of this family of faith.'
- Communion is an act of grace, communicating God's love, a symbol that can help the child experience acceptance and blessing.
- You have helped your child attain a basic understanding of what communion means. Your child now understands that communion is an act of remembering for those who love Jesus, not a snack to help him or her make it through worship!

You may decide for your child not to participate in communion for some of the following reasons:

- The tradition of our denomination has directed that communion follows baptism so that participants have dedicated themselves to the cross-bearing lifestyle of Jesus.
- It would be easy to trivialize communion by partaking without realizing or remembering the meaning, a risk for us all.
- It is a good discipline for our children to wait and anticipate the privilege of being a part of the communion experience with their church family after they are baptized."

Additional family discussions when children do make their personal profession of faith in Christ and are baptized can make the communion experience assume a whole different meaning as they understand the depth of the sacrifice Christ made for them.

Parenting Resources

Many parents will more readily consult a resource such as a book, video, DVD, or Web site because they can fit it into their schedule and "down time." A church that provides a library of parenting resources can be a great encourager of good parenting. Stay-at-home moms or dads could have book discussions during the day, facilitated by a seasoned parent or parents. Night book studies could be organized if there is sufficient interest and commitment from busy parents.

Appendix 4 provides a good "starter" list of printed resources for churches just beginning or updating their parenting library. New resources come out frequently, and sometimes parents will donate a resource they have purchased and completed. Not all parent resources are appropriate for all churches, so you may want to have a person or team that will evaluate and/or identify new resources to be purchased as well as assess donated resources.

Parent Support Groups

Some churches have discovered the value of parent support groups. The support groups may be organized around a special parenting need such as single parenting, parenting special needs children, parenting newborns, or another unique family issue. On the other hand, sometimes it helps to share common challenges of child rearing and faith nurturing with other parents on the same journey.

The support group may share common frustrations and offer solutions that have worked for them. Sometimes if the facilitator is a parent of grown children, the voice of successful survival is helpful to those in the midst of the journey. On-line discussions are a newer parenting help format, and might be a lifeline for parents that need immediate assistance or guidance.

A few churches have successfully matched younger parents with older parents in mentoring relationships. Much of the success depends on whether the parents have input into selecting their mentors. The church may encourage the relationships by scheduling meeting times and providing childcare for the children of the younger parents.

It Takes a Village...

Whatever parents identify as their needs, churches must encourage and support parents while providing strong, effective programming that supports the family's faith efforts for their children. The African proverb is true for the church too: "It takes a village to raise a child." For sure it takes a church to support families in raising their children to know and love God and others.

Notes

[1] According to A. C. Nielsen Company, children average twenty-eight hours per week of television viewing.

[2] David Elkind, *Ties That Stress: The New Family Imbalance* (Cambridge, Mass.: Harvard University Press, 1994), chapter 10.

[3] Shirley Morgenthaler, *Exploring Children's Spiritual Formation: Foundational Issues* (River Forest, Ill.: Pillars Press, Concordia University, 1999), 63–67.

[4] George Barna, *Transforming Children into Spiritual Champions* (Ventura, Calif.: Issachar Resources, 2003), 181.

[5] Diana Garland, *Sacred Stories of Ordinary Families: Living the Faith in Daily Life* (San Francisco: Jossey-Bass, 2003), 3.

CHAPTER 4

Does Your Church Value the Preschool and Grade-school Teachers and/or Leaders and Equip Them to Do a Very Important Ministry?

Quality and Quantity Matter

Enlistment of volunteer leaders is perhaps the most difficult and constant responsibility of childhood ministry. An effective ministry requires a massive labor force. Seldom does a church have the optimum number of adult teachers/leaders for all of its ministries with preschoolers and grade-schoolers. In smaller membership churches, the percentage of adult members needed for these younger age groups is quite large. The number of leaders required for quality teaching and safety is greater for the youngest members than for any other age group, and the number of children's events as well as adult events requiring childcare leadership seems to multiply each year in many churches.

Leaders are usually needed for the Bible study, discipleship, missions, and music ministries for the preschoolers and grade-schoolers. In addition, a church may have weekday preschool, full-day childcare, before- and after-school ministries, worship care ministries, children's worship, and other weekly or monthly ministries.

Some churches make a distinction between "teacher" and "leader." Sometimes they use the term "helper" to indicate someone who is not leading a group time. The reality of relating to preschoolers and grade-school children is that when an adult is with them, they are teaching either intentionally or unintentionally just through their interactions with the children. If a church assumes that everyone who is "with" preschoolers and grade-schoolers is teaching in some way, then "leaders" become more aware of their teaching role and perhaps are more intentional in their interactions as teaching opportunities. A church might decide to use the term "teacher" to indicate all of their adult leadership, and use distinctions such as "lead teacher" for the person in a classroom or ministry with primary teaching responsibility.

Recommended child per teacher ratios are lower for these younger age groups than for youth and adult groups. While adult leaders may be able to "take care" of more preschoolers or grade-schoolers than the recommended ratios given below, a congregation that takes seriously the faith formation of their preschoolers and grade-school children as well as the safety and protection of its minors and leadership must expect that the ratios be followed at all times in all ministries.

AGE GROUPING	ADULT/ CHILD RATIO	MAXIMUM GROUP SIZE
Babies–Kindergarten	1:3	12
Babies–Twos	1:3	12
Threes–Kindergarten	1:4	15
Babies	1:2	12
Ones–Twos	1:3	12
Threes–Pre-K	1:4	20
Kindergarten	1:5	24
Grade-school Children	1:6	26

One thriving church has large signs with the leader/child ratios posted outside the doors of the preschool rooms. When the maximum ratio is reached in a room, either another teacher must be put in the room, or preschoolers are turned away. They never violate their posted ratio. To some congregations that policy may seem legalistic and uninviting to families, but most parents of that church, both members and guests, actually perceive it as assurance that the church values their children. This policy also communicates to the teachers that their ministry will not be overwhelmed or compromised by poor planning on the part of ministry leadership or ministerial staff.

The Greatest Challenge: Leadership Enlistment

Perhaps the greatest challenge in childhood ministry today is finding, enlisting, and training adequate, committed leadership for preschoolers and grade-schoolers. Many churches settle for warm bodies or willing souls who already are overcommitted but just can't say, "No," because of guilt or perhaps because of their passion and concern for the ministry. The result of such a practice is often burnout on the part of potentially effective leaders, leaving the children with "caregivers" rather than teachers.

Guilt is too often the motivation used to enlist parents as teachers. The result is that parents "do their part," but their gifts and abilities may actually lie in other ministries. When that parent's children "age out" of preschool or grade-school, that leader is lost. Churches who rely heavily on parents as their preschool and grade-school leadership because it is their "duty" will experience a high rate of turnover and generally will have a poorer quality of teaching.

Some churches use teens to "fill in" when they do not have enough willing adult leaders. While using the reasoning that the youth *want* to "keep" the children, a church ministry can be less than it could be with committed adult teachers. Youth may be good at "babysitting," but what a church should be striving to do is to *teach* the children, not just care for them. In addition, youth need to be in their own ministries, growing in their faith. Another consideration is that often safety is compromised with teens whose judgment is not always as mature as is needed with young children. Some insurance companies will not apply liability insurance to teens under a certain age.

Other churches have resorted to rotating "workers" who will give one or two hours a month but will not accept a weekly teaching position. This practice is proving to be "unsettling" to children who do not know what to expect when they arrive at church. A number of issues present themselves with teaching situations in which leaders teach only one or two Sundays a month or even every other month:

- Because preschoolers and grade-schoolers learn about faith through relationships with people who strive to love them as Christ loves them, the practice of rotating leaders does not promote a strong bond between children and their teachers.
- Teachers who do not interact with the children weekly may miss important signals in a child's faith development that may need to be encouraged and explored over the following weeks.
- Good teaching is targeted to the needs of the pupils. Preschoolers, particularly, change so rapidly that lessons can miss the needs of the pupils if the teacher does not have regular contact with them and note their development.
- Expectations and discipline techniques vary greatly from person to person. Preschoolers and grade-schoolers are secure when they know what is expected from them. With a different teacher each week, children will constantly test limits because they may not remember what each teacher expects.
- Rotating leaders usually do not feel any responsibility for contacting absentees because they may not be aware of the attendance pattern. As a result, children may be absent for months before a caring teacher contacts them.
- Good teaching involves good planning. Rotating teachers often do not feel responsibility for planning quality teaching experiences, and in some cases do not have a copy of the literature if it is simply "passed around."

Another rotation model is gaining in popularity, but it has difficulties as well. This teaching model is used with grade-school children. With this model four teachers present the same lesson each Sunday, usually for a month, but to four different rotating groups of children. All the groups of children study the same biblical content for four Sundays, but they experience a method aimed at a different learning style each week. Proponents offer strong arguments for this rotation teaching model:

- Children have fun and learn through creative teaching methods geared for various learning styles. The methods are active and engaging, and each teacher can teach in his or her own learning style or interest area.
- Rotation is a time-saver for teachers. Teachers prepare one lesson, and teach it four or five times to a different group each week. Adjustments must be made for ability and thinking levels of different ages of children.
- Repetition ensures that children *really learn* ten to twelve Bible stories each year.
- The rotation format is very flexible.

While the rotation system is very appealing and convenient for busy adults, it has a number of serious problems for the children and the teaching-learning process:

- Relationships with teachers are not established when a class has a different teacher each week. Yet faith *is* relationship—a relationship with God. Children learn what God is like through people who themselves have faith in God. To understand what the Scriptures mean, children need to see the character of God reflected in the lives of God's people. This is the most important aspect of teaching children what faith means, even more important than the cognitive information.
- Learning biblical content and experiencing the content are the primary foci of rotation teaching. Life application and the learning of Bible messages woven throughout the lives of many Bible characters, not just one story, are not usually emphasized.
- Rotation teaching most often emphasizes a different learning style in each group each week. The children with that learning style enjoy the experience, but it does not appeal to the other children who do not have that learning style. Good teaching will always include a variety of activities that appeal to the different learning styles of all the children.
- Is "fun" always good teaching? When the method overpowers the message, what have the children really learned? For example, a theme or activity can be so visually and experientially stimulating that the experience or the fun is remembered rather than the important

biblical message. Good teaching uses engaging activities that invite a child to learn, apply, and internalize a biblical message or truth.

- Again, lack of consistency is asking for discipline problems with children. Each teacher has different behavioral expectations and levels of enforcement. When children do not know what is expected behaviorally from a teacher, they will test the limits.

Some churches have strengthened the typical teaching rotation system, but the modifications still involve considerable commitment on the part of the coordinator/minister as well as the teachers. Eight adult teachers per grouping are divided into four teams of two teachers each. Teams 1 and 2 teach for a quarter (3 months), then team 1 attends their adult class and team 3 joins team 2 for the second quarter. In the third quarter, team 2 returns to their adult class and team 4 joins team 3. In the final quarter, team 3 drops out and team 1 joins team 4. With this rotation model, each team of adults teaches for two quarters and is off two quarters.

- If a teacher needs to be absent one Sunday during his or her rotation, people on one of the other teams can be enlisted as a substitute.
- The children have one familiar team of teachers as well as one new team each quarter. That provides at least some continuity for the children who attend regularly.
- Irregular attendees could experience new teachers virtually each time they attend, potentially adding to their hesitancy to attend when their parents provide the opportunity.
- A coordinator must keep teaching teams informed and connected to the ministry during their period of teaching as well as during their time in their adult classes (when needed for substitution).

Building a Community of Exceptional Teachers and Leaders

What would your church give for a waiting list of people to teach or lead children? It is not a matter of what you would give, but rather, what would you do? Some churches do have a waiting list because they understand that an inspired and equipped cadre of leaders is a primary responsibility of the paid or volunteer ministry leader. Many of the preschool and grade-school leaders also are parents, grandparents, aunts, uncles, and neighbors to children in and out of the church family. The investment in the children's personal growth, knowledge, and skill can be applied in their relationships with children everywhere.

Churches with waiting lists start by building a community, not just filling slots.

1. Create written position expectations for each leadership position needed.

When a church has traditionally had teaching responsibilities "understood" rather than "written down," creating written position descriptions for each ministry situation is initially labor intensive. However, when people know what they are agreeing to do, they will be more likely to do it well because they know what the expectations are. Keep the descriptions somewhat general, but include the important aspects of each program.

2. Invite people to join you on a mission.

A minister or ministry leader can begin to build a community of people who understand and believe in investing in young lives. To do so, the leader will spend considerable time and energy in enlistment all year long, not just at the beginning of a new church year. Rather than viewing enlistment as a list to be conquered, see it as a ministry of finding gifts and abilities that people may not even know they have. People who find the right place to use their talents and interests, are equipped to serve effectively, and are encouraged and appreciated by the ministers often become passionate, committed teachers.

A word of caution to the minister: You are not enlisting people to help you. You are enlisting people to use their gifts and abilities to guide the children in their faith formation. Too often ministers or directors who are in charge of enlistment of leadership ask people to help them and take it personally when a person refuses to accept a position and just do the task themselves. When you as a leader do something that someone else could do (such as teaching a class or preparing a snack or organizing a resource closet), you are depriving someone else of the opportunity to use his or her abilities and time in service.

Enlistment is an art, but it takes on the personality of the enlister. Use these guidelines to assist you in developing your enlistment technique:

- Begin by praying for God to lead you to persons who are called and willing to respond to His call. God does not give us children without calling out leadership to teach them. Your responsibility is to identify those persons whom God is already calling out even before you approach them. Invite others to pray with you, to be your prayer support team.
- List the qualities of the person you are seeking for each position. Do not limit yourself to the many general qualities, such as love of children, rapport with children, dependability, willingness to learn, patience, and being a Christlike example. Look for the specific qualities you need for a position. The needs of the children, the teaching team, or the content of the teaching material may dictate some special requirements. For example, a class with special needs children, a new Christians' or inquirers' class, a music class, or a lead teacher position may indicate other qualities needed. Determine which qualities are absolute "musts" and those that might be developed.
- Look for people who have most of the qualities you listed. Look for people with growth potential in some areas you may have listed.

Be careful to seek out people who want to meet the many needs of preschoolers, older children, and their families. Sometimes we enlist people who volunteer simply to have their unfulfilled needs met. Emotionally unhealthy adults do not make the best teachers of the most vulnerable people in our congregations.

- Ask some of your best leaders for the names of people who they might recommend for leadership with preschoolers and grade-schoolers. You may not know some people in your church very well, and God can use others to "find" people who you did not know possessed just the qualities for which you were searching. I have had people to respond to prayer requests at prayer meetings, and they were people that I would not have identified as potential leaders with children. They proved to be exceptional leaders for many years.

- Depending on your church polity, share the names with the appropriate committee or coordinating group. In some larger churches, the ministerial staff is the coordinating group. If possible, avoid having multiple people approach the same person for various positions. Of course, they may turn down your needed position yet indicate an interest in another age group or ministry opportunity. If that is the case, you can share that person's interest with the appropriate ministry leader or enlistment coordinating group.

- When you are clear to proceed with the enlistment, call to set an appointment to discuss the ministry opportunity. A visit to the home is preferable. If the person works outside the home, a lunch appointment (with you buying the lunch) is another alternative. If you need to talk with them at church, choose a quiet place, and allow adequate time for the process. (Note: Avoid pulpit appeals, hallway coercion, or begging and pleading. From such casual and sometimes manipulative measures you will enlist resentful, guilt-ridden, and sometimes self-needy persons who will not be the most effective leaders for the preschoolers and/or grade-schoolers. If possible, avoid telephone enlistment, but sometimes schedules make this necessary.)

In talking with prospective leaders:

- Share why you chose them, including the information about the ministry position and the qualities you observe in them that make you think this may be a good match. You may take the literature they will be using for the teaching experience. Be sure to convey the importance of this position to the lives of preschoolers or grade-schoolers.

- Offer them an opportunity to observe the class or group that needs a teacher/leader.

- Describe training opportunities that will be available, and indicate your expectations for attendance. While you may not "require" attendance since they are volunteers, you will want to encourage them to agree to engage in some of the training opportunities available to make them stronger leaders.

- Allow some time for discussion. They most likely will have questions or concerns to which you need to respond. The more information they have, the more informed their response will be.
- Pray with each prospective leader. Ask him or her to continue praying about the position. Agree on a date you will call for a response. Most often, you would want to give a week.
- You should accept their immediate answer if they wish to give you one—either positive or negative. You may accept their answer if they know immediately that God is (and perhaps has been) calling them to this position. Even if they may seem negative about accepting the position, encourage them to pray about it before they give you a final answer, but accept graciously their decision of "yes" or "no" whenever they offer it to you. In later months or years, they may be in a position to accept a teaching assignment, and you want to leave good feelings so that they will be open to wherever God may lead them in the future.

3. Equip them to be effective in their positions.

Too often we enlist leadership and expect them to "sink or swim." Sometimes our expectations of them are idealistic rather than realistic. While it is important to have high expectations of the leadership, they are volunteers and must have a variety of learning opportunities throughout the year to be the best they can be. We often assume that they know various aspects of their ministry rather than insuring that they know it through training. Equipping events or experiences for the volunteers need to be both short "bytes" of learning as well as more extensive training sessions of several hours. Because teachers today are very busy, the training needs to fit the schedules of the leaders in your congregation. You will have better attendance if you choose training times that fit their schedule rather than yours. Be sure you invite only those people who will benefit from the particular training you have planned. Occasionally, you may have a training session for a particular group of teachers who have unique needs and challenges, such as special needs preschoolers or grade-schoolers, new teachers with no experience, missions or music teachers, or Bible study leaders.

Be creative in structuring your learning experiences. Multitudes of both traditional and innovative ways are available to engage your leaders in learning.

Meetings

The most common form of a training event is a meeting. However, remember that the meeting is for their benefit, not yours. With that in mind, make it worth their time, and make it enjoyable. You want to make it more likely that they will choose to attend another training event in the future because of the usefulness of this meeting.

Be creative in scheduling. Some churches are providing equipping opportunities early Sunday morning before Sunday school, during a Wednesday evening churchwide meal, immediately following the Sunday morning worship service (with a family meal and childcare included), a Friday evening meal and learning experience at the home of the minister, or other appealing times and settings. Ask the teachers what time best suits their schedules and family needs.

Consider some of these suggested meeting or individualized learning designs as you plan learning opportunities for your leadership:

- Start with *pre-service training* during which they are prepared for their ministry. Make this more than an orientation to the teaching space and materials. Build on the classroom observation you offered them in the enlistment process. Provide one or more learning sessions that inform them about the age group they will teach; the safety, security, and hygiene policies of the church; the teaching methodology; how to do ministry with their group of children and visitors; and other basic information.
- Short *learning experiences* can be scheduled with all of the teachers or with targeted groups or teams of teachers. Short learning experiences usually get larger participation than long ones. Thirty-minute to one-hour sessions at convenient times could give information and assistance for preschool teachers in
  - ~ first aid tips
  - ~ ways to guide behavior
  - ~ creative ideas for any one of the activity areas (learning centers)
  - ~ how to do group time with 3s, 4s, and kindergarteners
  - ~ use of the Bible in the activity areas
  - ~ contents and use of the resource room
  - ~ learning preschool songs to use for teaching
  - ~ tips for visiting preschoolers in their homes
  - ~ storytelling techniques
  - ~ teaching resources such as books and videos
- Teachers of grade-schoolers might have short learning experiences about
  - ~ attractive bulletin board or focal wall ideas
  - ~ using drama with children
  - ~ talking with a child about salvation
  - ~ guiding behavior (discipline)
  - ~ creative cards and letters to send to children

~ Bible skill games and activities
~ guiding children in prayer experiences
~ using music as a teaching method
~ storytelling techniques
~ resources such as books and videos

• *Conference calls* are emerging as another training vehicle. An expert in a particular subject could be engaged. Teachers could then call a prearranged number for a group connection. While it has some disadvantages, many people who are very comfortable with technology and use it in their work find this method very convenient and cost-effective. However, with some newer plans, the cost for the telephone call is the caller's responsibility. Local phone calls, though, usually involve no charge.

• W*ritten training* is a quick way to assist teachers and encourage them to be continuous learners.

~ Short articles from magazines or the Internet may be reproduced (needing permission from the magazines), or the contents may be summarized and handed or mailed to teachers with the encouragement to read them. Be sure to evaluate any online or magazine articles to ensure that they are in agreement with your educational philosophy and your church's theology.

~ Teaching literature often carries teaching tips that could be creatively marked as noteworthy so that teachers read them.

~ Newsletters can have training articles and suggestions.

~ Teachers can be e-mailed a link to an appropriate article on a Web site. An original article with training content is effective as well. A book review or extra teaching ideas could be communicated through e-mail, too.

• *Mentoring* of new teachers by experienced teachers is a very effective method of getting novices quickly taught. The one-on-one relationship is highly effective even with adult education! Sometimes the minister or director may be the mentor of a group of teachers in a class for a month or a quarter.

• Provide *resources for individualized learning.* Books (especially short ones), videos, DVDs, CD-ROMs and other resources that leaders can fit into their own schedules can be highly effective for some people. They need to be kept in a place that is visible to the teachers so that they will be reminded to take advantage of the resources. Some ministry leaders make a point of recommending certain ones to individuals who need some extra help in areas that may be covered in the resource.

• Schedule *potential leader classes* annually. Do not wait until you are desperate for leaders. Discover and develop new preschool and grade-school leadership throughout the year as you enlist regular program substitutes, recruit vacation Bible school leadership, and cultivate relationships with parents and new members. When the time comes to conduct the potential leader class for preschool and grade-school leadership, you will have a list of names to invite personally in addition to the open invitation to the congregation.

4. Meet teachers' personal needs as growing Christians

Sometimes teachers of preschoolers and grade-schoolers are not motivated, encouraged, or even challenged to continue their adult faith journey. Rather than reflecting on the meaning of the biblical content, missions challenge, or other teaching content to their lives, they often consider only its relevance for the children's lives.

While that perspective is necessary for effective teachers, they also need to be encouraged to engage in in-depth personal Bible study or perhaps group studies. The best teachers of preschoolers and grade-schoolers teach from a well of knowledge and experience involving biblical truths and application, rather than from a minimal "cup" of knowledge they prepare simply for the teaching experience.

To develop that depth of knowledge, some churches are finding that their preschool and grade-school teachers are requesting to rotate by months or weeks with another team of teachers so they can experience adult study on a regular basis and to maintain relationships with those in their adult classes or groups. However, while that may meet the needs of the adults, it is detrimental to the children who need consistency and relationship to feel secure and connected as well as to develop significant relationships that reflect the dependable and caring nature of God.

More effective ways to encourage the spiritual growth of teachers of preschoolers and grade-schoolers include the following:

- Expecting preschool and grade-school leaders to teach only once a week rather than in multiple ministries. If teachers are given the opportunity to participate in some adult experiences at church, they will have some of their needs met as well.
- Providing a workshop for the teachers during which various approaches to personal Bible study could be presented and demonstrated. For example, it might include a format for studying how God worked in the lives of Bible personalities or for tracing certain Bible words/concepts through various passages. Bible study resources, including recommended books, might be introduced and made available for check out.
- Offering a monthly meeting at a convenient time (preferably occurring when other meetings are scheduled or immediately before or after significant church events). During this time, a strong Bible teacher might lead in an adult Bible study focusing on the Bible content that

will be taught to the preschoolers and/or grade-schoolers. This is especially effective if all of the classes are teaching the same biblical content and using the same publisher of literature.

- Encouraging a Bible study or personal growth opportunity with other adults on Sunday evening, in small groups throughout the week, or once a month.
- Inviting preschool and grade-school children's teachers especially to be a part of adult experiences such as a special Bible study, a mission project, a prayer group, or another small group experience.

5. Show appreciation to teachers, and build community between the teachers as well as with the rest of the church.

Another reason adults want to rotate teaching preschoolers and/or grade-schoolers (or not teach at all) is because they feel isolated from their adult friends. If they teach children more than once a week when adult groups also are meeting, they tend to feel disconnected and often "put upon," although they may have great passion and calling in their ministry. Remember that most leadership of preschoolers and grade-schoolers are volunteers unless it is weekday preschool, full-day childcare, or before- and after-school care ministries. While most teachers minister without expecting recognition, the wise leader will encourage volunteers by expressing appreciation often and giving special affirmation periodically.

You can show appreciation in many creative ways for the preparation, commitment, and dependability of volunteers as well as the paid weekday staff:

- Send notes or e-mails when you observe a special teaching moment or an extra effort from a teacher.
- Send birthday cards, electronic cards, or have birthday celebrations quarterly honoring the teachers with birthdays.
- Periodically leave small gifts (candy bars, bedding plants, decorative soap, gum, etc.) with a thank-you note for their service.
- Have a special teacher appreciation Sunday or week with events that show appreciation.
- Engage children and parents in "surprising" teachers with expressions of appreciation.
- Involve teachers' Sunday school classes or other adult small groups in honoring those who are "in service" members of their group. They also might be provided with a prayer calendar with teachers' names.
- Encourage Sunday school classes or other adult small groups to send preschool and grade-school teachers a special invitation to their "social" events.
- Remind the church through Web sites, newsletter articles, pulpit presentations, and other communication avenues of the importance of the value of the service of these volunteers.

- Provide names of substitutes for teachers so that they can be gone when it is necessary. A few churches that have year-round programming offer one month a year (usually during the summer) for teachers to have a break. This bonus requires that other leaders who might not be willing to teach for the entire year might teach one month.

6. Provide teachers with the resources they need to be excellent teachers.

In many churches, the budget for teaching supplies and other resources is so minimal that teachers often buy their own supplies. That can present a number of problems:

- Some teachers do not have the financial resources to buy the teaching supplies they need to be creative and effective. Word spreads rapidly, and soon these people and other potential leaders will not teach because of their personal financial issues.
- Teachers who buy their own supplies resent anyone else "using up" what they bought, and so they resort to locked cabinets or become negative toward other leaders. This does not present a very positive role model for the children to whom we are trying to teach generosity and sharing.
- Teachers resort to teaching methods that do not require any materials. Most often they use the lecture method, not a very effective or inviting method for helping children learn.
- Teachers may make poor choices and purchase materials that are not safe or appropriate.

One way we demonstrate that teachers are valued is that we give them the resources they need to do effective teaching. A resource room, closet, or even shelves where common expendable supplies can be kept for teachers to restock the teaching materials in their rooms can save them time and encourage creative teaching. Following are some basic expendable supplies.

For all ages
- Construction paper in a variety of colors (pay attention to seasonal colors)
- Drawing or manila paper of various sizes
- Safety scissors for children, and teacher scissors
- Washable paint in a variety of colors
- Large paint brushes
- Masking tape
- Zip lock bags in various sizes for storing resource items
- Envelopes
- Newspaper
- Sentence strip paper

- Pads of chart paper
- Bulletin board paper or cloth (if the rooms have bulletin boards)
- Dry erase markers (if the rooms have dry erase boards)
- Tissues
- Postcards for absentees
- Paper towels
- Rolls of white paper such as butcher paper

Preschoolers
- Large crayons
- A collection of pictures from magazines, separated by topic (a senior adult might cut these from magazines donated to the church)
- Waxed paper
- Disposable gloves for diaper changing
- Paint smocks or men's shirts
- Play dough

Grade-school children
- Washable markers in a variety of colors
- Paper clips
- Pencils
- Staplers
- Poster board
- Index cards in various sizes
- Small paintbrushes
- Brad fasteners
- Clay

By purchasing in quantity, bulk prices can save the church money, and teachers' time is saved as well. In addition to these basic supplies, the teachers can request supplies in sufficient time for the minister or coordinator to purchase them before the teaching session in which they will be used. Such resource areas become disorganized and depleted rather quickly, so one person should be responsible for purchasing and maintaining the resources. This person needs to be a layperson who enjoys being of assistance to others and is a gifted organizer.

Resource room or closet

Some churches have a larger area for resources. Often it is a room or at least a spacious closet. These resource rooms have quantities of the expendable supplies, but they also have other teaching materials and seasonal resources available. Some resource rooms have laminators, die-cut machines, and copiers, but ministries that cannot afford such equipment still can have resources that encourage teachers to vary their sensory materials for learning experiences.

Preschool resource rooms often provide a variety of teaching pictures, puzzles, books, appropriate toys for the activity areas, dress-up clothes, rhythm instruments, and other teaching items that can be rotated depending on the lesson, the season, and the teaching suggestions.

Grade-school children's teachers need things such as Bible times costumes, maps, Bible skill games, musical instruments, and clipboards from time to time. The resource room or closet can be as small or large as you have space, personnel, and money to develop.

Teacher priority

The most significant element of any learning experience is the teacher, so we need to give priority attention to securing the best teachers for the preschoolers and grade-schoolers, training them to become excellent teachers, and encouraging them to grow in their faith so that they are effective examples of Christ followers for the preschoolers and grade-schoolers they are teaching.

CHAPTER 5

Does Your Church Minister to Children with Special Needs and Situations?

Churches seeking to meet needs of families in their community often have not considered that some of the children and families have a special need for the ministry that a loving church family can provide. Sometimes we unwittingly "shut out" people from our ministry because we do not see the need and therefore do not provide for it. It is legitimate to argue that every church cannot meet every need, but at least we can be sensitive to people who may have special needs that are not being addressed by any other congregation and consider whether this church has the desire, resources, and leadership to be the church that will minister to them.

Special needs that churches often overlook include physical and mental disabilities, economic and social barriers, single-parent families, or special language groups.

Children with Physical and/or Mental Disabilities

Most often churches do not provide for persons with special physical or mental needs until one is born into one of the church families or someone becomes aware of a family in the community in need of ministry. Yet thousands of families have children with disabilities. Many are not attending any church because there isn't "a place" for them. These families are often stressed not only in the ways all families experience stress, but also by finances and intense caregiving for their special needs children.

To commit to this special ministry, a church first must determine if it can do it effectively. You would not want to start without careful evaluation and preparation.

1. Form a team or committee to consider the community needs as well as the church resources and interest in ministry to children with physical and/or mental disabilities. Use the existing ministry team that coordinates the preschool and/or grade-school ministry (see chapter 12), or form a new team for this exploration phase.

2. The minister and/or team should survey the community, town, or city to discover which churches already are providing ministry to children with special physical or mental needs. Some church weekday preschool programs or full-day childcare programs may have disabled children who attend other church ministries on Sunday or throughout the week, but sometimes they do not. In addition, call the county or city government agency that services families of children with disabilities and find out what the population statistics are for disabled children in your ministry area.

3. Acquire books, videos, and other resources that will help you identify what needs you might prepare to meet in your ministry. Most preschoolers with disabilities attend regular preschools that have teachers prepared for dealing with their unique needs. Some grade-school children with disabilities are taught within existing school classes (mainstreaming), but others may be in special classes that can help them maximize their potential. Your church may be able to minister to some grade-school children with disabilities within your existing classes, but you may not have the facilities or leadership to begin an extensive ministry without additional resources. Discuss with others what God may be calling your church to do well. Your state or local denominational judicatory may have resources available that will guide you step by step in determining what you want to do or perhaps realistically can do.

4. Prepare a detailed proposal, and gain approval or "blessing" from the appropriate church committees, teams, or church decision-making bodies to begin preparing for the ministry.

5. Enlist the leadership, using good enlistment practices. Be sure that these teachers have a heart for this ministry and are especially patient, caring people. Proper training also is essential.

6. Train the leadership, including information unique to the disabilities, and instruct them in the literature that will be used.

7. Plan your strategy for informing potential families of children with disabilities, using the agencies you have already contacted in the exploration stage and contacts within the church family as well. You may want to let other churches know of your ministry so they will be informed enough to refer families that could benefit from your ministry to your church.

Children with Economic Needs

Churches often fail to minister to children from a lower socio-economic group. Many times these children are in the church neighborhood that perhaps has changed in recent years. By his own pronouncement, Jesus was sent to "preach good news to the poor" as well as "proclaim freedom for the prisoners / and recovery of sight for the blind, / to release the oppressed, / to proclaim the year of the Lord's favor" (Lk. 4:18–19).

Jesus' mission in the world is ours as his followers. We can offer excuses as to why others need to minister to these children, but God has placed them in our midst. The church's Great Commission directive is to begin in "Jerusalem," each church's local mission field. Responsive churches understand that creative programming and staffing may need to replace their current ministry plans.

Consideration should be given to whether the church will go to the children or whether the children/families will be brought to the church building. The purpose of reaching the children is to minister; taking them to the church building is not the only measure of ministry. It might prove more effective in reaching more children to provide a program in the community. A weekday ministry one afternoon a week after school in the neighborhood might be the best approach. Observe your community to determine when children seem to be most available.

Sometimes a church may decide that bringing the children to the church building would be the best approach. The leaders need to know how to respond to the challenge of children who have not experienced the expected church culture behavior. The children will have little Bible knowledge and may even have misinformation from a variety of cultural sources. However, the joy of experiencing the impact of Christlike relationships as the gospel is communicated in inviting ways is immeasurable.

Not only will you need to provide hands-on learning activities and caring, prepared leaders, but also you will need to ready the entire congregation as part of the support system for such a ministry. This might include preparing the children already involved in your ministry, their parents, as well as those not directly related to the ministries. Your senior pastor needs to be fully supportive and publicly encouraging. Any governing boards, committees, or teams must give their blessing and support as well to remove potential barriers to a successful ministry.

Children come from families who also need to hear and experience the gospel from Christ followers. Seriously consider ministry to the whole family, not just the children. God wants families to nurture their children "in the way they should go," and a church that impacts a family's life profoundly multiplies the influence God can have on the lives of their children. When all of the groundwork, training, and preparation have been completed, begin contacting the children, and watch involved lives become transformed.

Children of Single Parents

Children of single parents might also need special consideration in your ministry. One-fourth of all children under the age of 18 live with a single parent, and one-third of all children born in the United States each year are born to an unmarried female.[1] What a mission field, an extraordinary opportunity for ministry in every community!

Parenting is challenging with two parents, but single moms and dads as well as their children need encouragement and assistance so their children can become all that God intends for them to be. Many single-parent families are especially struggling with time, energy, and financial issues; and those resource limitations need to be considered in ministry with them.

Because many of the children visit in an alternating schedule between their parents, they may miss more programs than some of the other children. This makes it difficult for the children to establish relationships and provides a built-in excuse for them not to attend at all. If teachers are aware of the irregular attendance patterns, they can intentionally "buddy" them with another child and promote their contact through the telephone and e-mail communication in between programming. Encouraging our children to be concerned about each other is an important teaching that is very Christlike.

If a church decides to minister to the children as well as their single parents, a single-adult ministry can be developed by the adult and children's staff or leadership. From a myriad of possibilities, the ministry for the children can include providing activities when their parents are meeting, forming a support group for the children if you have leaders with special training in children of divorce, or coordinating a "babysitting co-op" of people who will give the single parent a respite by taking care of his or her children for an evening. Children who have only one parent active in their lives may need a male or female "parent substitute" to fill the need they have for the influence of both genders.

Children from Language Churches/Missions

Some churches have language groups or mission churches that they sponsor or support. While some language churches provide their own preschool and grade-school children's ministry, many others include their youngsters in the preschool and grade-school programming of the sponsoring church. In many cases, the preschoolers speak the language the parents speak in the home, so it is helpful to have a bilingual teacher or at least a floating assistant to help with communication.

Often the grade-school children are bilingual and can function quite well in the church ministry because of their school experiences. However, to be the kind of support these children need, teachers need to be aware of the cultural customs of the parents. Language increasingly becomes a potential barrier between parent and child if the parents are not fluent in English. It is important to be sensitive and respectful of parents who may not be able to speak English very well but are very competent and caring parents. If communication is a problem, usually someone in the language church can assist.

If a language group or mission has its own preschool and grade-school children's ministry, they may need assistance in organizing the ministry and training the teachers. They may actually need some teachers from the sponsoring church until they can "get on their feet." They also may need help in securing furniture, equipment, and teaching materials. Giving them your "cast offs" may not be the best choice if you want to convey the love and respect Jesus has for them, but assisting in whatever ways you can is paramount.

If you are sharing space with this ministry, you will need to establish policies about shared space as well as inform them of church policies regarding safety and security (see chapters 7 and 10). This concept will be difficult for many of them to accept. Few cultures have as many rules and regulations as Americans do, but it is important that all ministries using the church facilities follow the same policies.

World missions have come to our doorstep, and now we can serve in Christ's name to all nations without leaving our own community. What an opportunity God has given all of us.

Notes

[1] *Census Bureau On Line,* www.childstats.gov.

CHAPTER 6

Does Your Church Have an Intentional, Appropriate Process for Guiding Children into a Personal Relationship with Jesus Christ?

In an evangelical church last Sunday a shy but courageous child made her way down the seemingly endless aisle of the worship center. The pastor leaned down and took her hand. "Hi, Julie," the sensitive pastor greeted her. "What do you want to tell me this morning?"

"I want to join the church," Julie responded almost in a whisper.

How that pastor, the parents, and the church responded in that moment was crucial for Julie.

Fortunately, salvation is the work of the Holy Spirit. We can trust the Holy Spirit to enter that child's life at just the right moment. Our role as God's nurturers in this holy work is to prepare the way by teaching, modeling, guiding, and encouraging children in our care. We also must seek to understand how God created children to have a unique way of thinking that will change with age.

The people in Julie's life had prepared her for this crucial moment. Julie's parents had been laying the faith foundations in their home since the day she was born. Her teachers at church, too, had taught her basic biblical truths, had been sensitive to her probing questions, and had built caring relationships with her for ten years. The pastor had thoughtfully decided how he would counsel children who responded to the public invitation or asked to counsel with him privately. Julie's parents had attended several classes offered at their church on how to assist Julie in her faith journey and had been talking with her as she grew in her understanding. They perceived that the Holy Spirit was convicting Julie, and they had been praying for this day; but they were careful not to pressure Julie by their desires, knowing this was a crucial life decision for Julie. Even though Julie's parents have the primary responsibility of nurturing her faith, her teachers, her ministers, and her church could prayerfully guide Julie at this crucial moment.

Before the Decision

The spiritual guidance given a child from her earliest years is critical. Rather than indoctrination, guidance will provide the child with a growing relationship with God through Godlike relationships with the important people in her life and the teaching that they impart. The earliest "faith foundation block" is trust. The ability to trust is firmly established in the first year of life as infants learn whether "their world" is trustworthy. As caregivers, especially parents, care for their needs, they establish trust. As others, such as teachers at church and other important caregivers also prove to be trustworthy, infants' ability to trust is strengthened, and they become hopeful people.

The establishment of trust is crucial not only to life in general, but particularly to a personal relationship with God. Young children experience life almost exclusively through their senses; yet they cannot see, hear, touch, smell, or see God. Therefore, they begin to "know God" as they experience the godly people in their lives who teach and live the character of God, as imperfect as it may be. Later, as children's ability to think abstractly emerges, they are able to relate to God in a more direct, personal way.

A church that values faith formation will give attention to teaching babies through trustworthy care and loving interactions that nurture their perceptions that "church is a good place to be, and the people here care for me." It is more than a "nursery" where babies are "tended." It must be an interactive care and teaching experience for the most basic concepts of love, appreciation for God's world, and other aspects of our faith that begin quite early.

Recent brain research has verified what many experienced teachers and observant parents have "known" for years. Only about 25 percent of the infant's "brain cells" are connected or "wired" at birth, although the full number are present at birth.[1] Through sensory experiences with others, the brain cells become actually connected so that by the end of the preschool years, much of the child's brain is "wired." How important it is, then, for a faith community to give attention to children's preschool learning and experiences, as it is the basic wiring for the rest of their lives?

As infants grow into young children, they will experience and learn about God primarily from the adults who guide them. Strong concepts about God, Jesus, the Bible, prayer, worship, and other faith basics are best learned in the early years through methods that relate to a child's life and development. Massive memorization does not insure learning. Powerful knowledge and retention occurs as the preschooler encounters learning related to his or her life experiences. This learning often happens through play as the child explores the world through imagination and application and as he or she learns Bible verses related in meaningful ways to those experiences.

Preschoolers and younger grade-schoolers who have had spiritual nurturing as an integral part of their home and church lives will have times when they will respond with feelings of love toward God. Those moments will be the basis on which they can move toward a life commitment when later the Holy Spirit convicts them of their sins and they can respond with repentance and belief to a loving and faithful God. Adults must be cautious not to "read" more into their loving responses, viewing them from our perspective rather than theirs. That loving response may be prompted by people rather than the Holy Spirit. If they are pressured to "make a decision" because *we* convict them rather than the Holy Spirit, they may become confused or make a "false decision" to please a person rather than God.

In addition, children often "adopt" the faith of parents or their faith families. They also adopt political parties, sports teams, and hobbies embraced by their friends or family. Adopted faith is an important step toward a full relationship with God, but it is not the fullest expression of being reconciled to God. Too often we "settle" for adopted faith in children when we need to continue guiding them into their own, fully embraced faith.

We must believe that the Holy Spirit is capable of working in the lives of children. They are granted a God-given will to respond or rebel to God's working in their lives. While that is a difficult idea to embrace for those of us who have chosen to be Christ followers, it is the same choice that we were given. As important as it is to us for the children to make the same choice, we must let God do God's work while we are faithfully nurturing our children to respond to God favorably.

The power they experience needs to be God's power, not ours. Manipulating a child to do what we want them to do is not a conversion decision, so careful guidance of a child needs to be as free as possible from external coercion. At the same time, being overly cautious can be too passive. Children still need adults to guide and interpret meaning but not to pressure them into doing something that God is not leading them to do.

God can do God's work in the life of a child or anyone of any age whenever God chooses. There is not "an age" when all children "are ready" for a variety of reasons and factors. However, through natural conversations with children about the ways God is working in your life as well as theirs, and through teaching of God's truths, children will know the "voice of God" when the time comes.

We know from adult recollections that for some children, repentance and acceptance of a new way of living are as natural as taking the next step. They often cannot say exactly when that time was. For others it will be a struggle or at least a momentous surrender that is clearly marked in their memories with a date and time. What we do know for sure is that children are capable of responding to God on many levels; and the parent, minister, teacher, or other adult responsibility is to be the presence of God in their midst and point them in the direction that they need to go (Prov. 22:6).

Issues in Conversion Counseling with Children

Julie's pastor always counsels with children individually. He knows that children mature very differently and are ready to make a conversion decision at various ages. This wise pastor has decided that he will have a private visit with every child. Julie's church also has a childhood minister, and the childhood minister counsels with the child as well. Only after both ministers have talked individually with a child and the parents will they confirm the child's decision to the congregation.

As a result of the discussion(s) with the child, the pastor and/or childhood minister might present the child for church membership and/or baptism; or they might suggest that the child attend an inquirer's class first. Perhaps the parents and pastor (or childhood minister) need to continue dialoguing with the child if they perceive that the child has taken a "step toward God" but may be responding to pressures other than the Holy Spirit.

In faith traditions unlike Julie's church, children may be baptized as infants and later "confirmed" at a certain age after completing a course of study. Whatever the faith tradition for becoming a Christ follower, every home and congregation has a responsibility to guide a child to make his or her own choice about repentance, forgiveness, and reconciliation with God to live his or her life in sync with God's desires.

When counseling a child about a conversion decision, a parent, minister, or other adult needs to consider the following child development issues:

- Children are egocentric at this age, even though we are guiding them to be other-centered. They must be able to give up their own will for God's will. They need to be able to give up their own wants in lieu of another's desires before they can make this life change.
- Grade-school children become very interested in belonging to groups comprised of peers or adults whose relationships are important to them—clubs, teams, neighborhood alliances, etc. Sometimes they will indicate that they want to "join the church" to feel they "belong" rather than as an indication of their desire to be reconciled to God. They often follow their peers as well if the leader(s) begins this process.
- Sometimes when children ask faith questions, especially those related to Jesus' death and resurrection, parents and ministers assume that the questions indicate readiness. It may be that they are ready, but it also may mean that they are simply gathering the information so that they can process it later. It is wise to answer the questions and perhaps go one step beyond their questions to test the interest. They will let you know whether to keep going or whether to stop and give the information time to incubate.
- Children desire love and attention from adults. If they observe other children receiving affirmation for their decision, they may seek to secure the same attention, but without understanding the meaning of

the decision made by the other child. They also may want to please an adult such as a parent, pastor, grandparent, or teacher. We must remember that it isn't about their doing what we want, but about their responding to what God wants.

- Children think differently from adolescents or adults. For example, they believe in magic—words and actions can cause certain things to happen. They often don't understand cause-and-effect very well so they ascribe certain actions or thoughts to actions that occur. While this happens with divorce, death, and catastrophes, sometimes it happens with conversion. If they answer the questions correctly or if they repeat the "sinner's prayer," then some children think they have "received salvation" when, in truth, they have not given their lives to Christ at all. After all, the "sinner's prayer" sounds like magical words to a child (as well as some adults, perhaps).

- Another way that children think differently is that they are literal thinkers before about the age of 12 years. Christianity is loaded with symbolism; but when we use symbolic terms with children, they do not understand their meaning. For example, "Give your heart to Jesus," is a symbolic phrase. We do not mean to literally "give your heart"; it is a symbol for our life or our will. Even if we explain the meaning to children, they can tell you what you said; but they don't understand the connection. So the words we use to talk with children are very important to their understanding of the concepts.

- Children must be able to understand the basics of the gospel message of redemption. Just "loving Jesus" is not enough. It is enough for younger children, but there must come a time that they understand their relationship to God in terms of repentance, forgiveness, and restoration.

Classes to Assist Parents and Children

Julie's church provides classes led by the childhood minister. They include information about some of the issues raised above plus guidance in how preschoolers' and grade-schoolers' faith forms. They give additional guidance in how to answer a child's questions and how to explain the gospel message to one's child using Scriptures. Books are recommended and placed in the parent library for anyone to read and apply to their child's spiritual journey. Julie's parents felt prepared to talk with Julie as her faith grew to this decisive point, and they trusted the Holy Spirit, with their nurturing and support, to do God's work in Julie's life.

Some congregations also provide "inquirer's classes" for children who may be asking questions but may need someone to guide them through some of the basics before they fully understand the gospel message for their lives. Other churches require that all children of a certain age go through such instruction so they will have all of the pertinent information and understanding when the Holy Spirit convicts and invites.

Conversion Counseling Suggestions

When a pastor or childhood minister counsels a grade-school child, he or she needs to determine several things:

- Is this child responding to the prompting of the Holy Spirit or to an external influence?
- Is the child initiating the process or is an anxious parent, grandparent, or other adult pushing the child to become anxious as well?
- Does the child relate his or her sins to God or to disobedience to other people such as parents, friends, the community, etc.?
- Does the child understand the basic gospel truths that determine his or her relationship to God?
- Does the child understand that this is a decision that affects his or her life from now on as he or she becomes a Christ follower?

Keeping those overarching questions in mind, Julie's childhood minister used these guidelines for counseling Julie:

Ask questions that require more than a "yes" or "no" response.

When you ask such questions such as, "Do you know you are a sinner?" or, "Do you want to become a Christian?" children know the answer you expect and may not understand the meaning of the question or the significance of the answer.

Instead, ask questions that will encourage children to express personal ideas and feelings. Ask questions such as, "What is sin?" "Who should be baptized and why?" or, "When did you first start thinking about joining the church?"

When you ask, "What do you mean when you say that you want to be baptized?" you are allowing them to tell you in their own words what they understand and what they want to do. When they verbalize their thoughts using their words, you are in a better position to clarify misunderstandings or pinpoint their motivation. If they cannot answer simple questions that do not have memorized answers, perhaps they need more information or more time to understand the importance of this decision.

Use terminology that children can understand.

We often use words that children do not understand at their stage of mental development. We need to use literal words rather than symbolic ones. Children younger than 12 years of age better understand "give your life to Jesus" rather than "give your heart to Jesus." The words *lost* and *saved,* as well as the use of bracelets or books of colors to symbolize the plan of salvation confuse rather than clarify a child's understanding. Instead, use an easy-to-understand translation of the Bible as you point out appropriate Scriptures to explain God's wonderful plan of salvation.

Help the child to understand the difference between an internal experience and an external expression.

Many children frequently equate conversion with baptism. The reason is obvious. Children usually see the two together. They respond best to what they can see, and one cannot see salvation. Be sure that the child understands that baptism is an act of obedience for those who already have repented and asked Jesus to come into their lives. Stress that baptism or joining the church will not make you a Christian.

Fear tactics or coercive methods must be avoided at all cost!

Frightening an impressionable child into a decision does not communicate that God is a God of love who died to redeem us. Also, scare tactics may cause the child to do "something" based on wrong motives. Manipulation, fear, power, or coercion from adults interferes with the work of the Holy Spirit. Going through the motions or saying the right words does not save anyone. A repentant, changed life lived in response to God is the desired decision.

The author was the program leader for a pastors' regional Monday morning gathering for support and continuing education. After a presentation much as this one, a young pastor came to me to talk privately about his son, who was five-years-old when he "accepted Jesus." After this information, he became concerned that perhaps his son had not known what he was doing, although the father/pastor insisted that there wasn't any coercion.

After acknowledging that God can do what God wants, I asked a few more questions before the pastor mentioned incidentally that he had prayed every night by his son's bed for his salvation. This well-meaning parent did not perceive that as "pressure"; but to a child, wanting to please Daddy, that was repeated pressure every night of his young life. Only God knows the meaning of that child's response, but we must be sensitive to how children respond to the adults who have such power for good or harm in their lives.

Don't press for an instant response.

Provide the opportunity for a response, but do not be disappointed if the child is not yet ready. Be sensitive, and remember it is God's work. God will be faithful in the life of that child. Also respect the God-given privilege of each person to make this personal decision—even children.

If the child is not ready to make a decision, affirm the child and the child's spiritual journey and discovery.

Pray for him or her daily. Continue regular dialogue with the child who has had a response to God in his or her life. Encourage the child to continue learning and listening for the voice of God in his or her life. Julie's parents and ministers together concluded that Julie understood the basics of the gospel as well as her need to make this personal life decision. Julie will attend the next new member's class for children, and her parents and teachers will continue discipling Julie for years to come.

Basic Counseling Model

Finding Scriptures for counseling people about their conversion decision is not difficult. The Bible is packed full of stories and Scriptures about reconciling our sinful selves to God's desires for our lives. However, some are better for children because of their concrete rather than symbolic meanings. You can mark your Bible by writing the first Scripture reference in the front of the Bible you plan to use, along with the page number. At the top of the first Scripture page, write the point of that verse (see phrases by bullets below). Highlight the verse or part of the verse you will use; then write the second scripture verse and page number at the bottom of that first page. On the second scripture's page, do the same thing, and continue throughout. The next Scripture is always at the bottom of the page if you progress in order.

Here are some Scriptures and dialogue you might want to include in your counseling sessions with children. Let the child guide you as he or she may ask questions or respond to your comments.

God loves you.

> *"This is love: not that we loved God, but that he loved us and sent his Son" (1 Jn. 4:10).*

Children need to know that God loves them more than anyone, even their parents. Talk about God's great love for all people, including that child. God made people to be in relationship with God, and God made people in God's image. God loves us so much that God wants us to have the very best life possible. That is why God tells us how to live to have the happiest life.

Sin separates us from God.

> *"For the wages of sin is death, but the gift of God is eternal life in Christ Jesus our Lord" (Rom. 6:23).*

Explain what "wages" are if they don't know (payment for working, like the money their parents receive for their jobs). Describe how God told Adam and Eve they could eat from every tree in the garden of Eden except the tree that was in the middle of the garden, but they chose to disobey God and eat from the forbidden tree. When we live the way we choose to live instead of the way God wants us to live, that is sin. Explain that when people sin, the payment is death of who they are inside (their souls) instead of living forever with God as God planned for us to do. God sent Jesus to pay for people's sins so they can live forever with God.

Everyone sins and deserves to be punished.

> *"For all have sinned and fall short of the glory of God" (Rom. 3:23).*

Everyone who has ever lived has chosen to live their way instead of God's way, so they have sinned. "Fall short" means to not be able to be as good as God is all by ourselves, so we deserve to receive the punishment of death for our sins.

Christ paid your punishment for sin.

> *"But God demonstrates his own love for us in this: While we were still sinners, Christ died for us" (Rom. 5:8).*

God still loves us so much, even when we sin and are being disobedient to God, that God sent Jesus, God's only Son, to die in our place. Jesus never sinned, so he shouldn't have died, but Jesus took everyone's place who has sinned, is sinning, or ever will sin. But Jesus didn't stay dead. He came back to life and lives even today with God.

Be sorry for your sin.

> *"If we confess our sins, [God] is faithful and just and will forgive us our sins and purify us from all unrighteousness" (1 Jn. 1:9).*

"Confess" means to be honestly sorry for your sin and to agree with God that you sinned. God knows you have sinned, but you must admit to God that you have sinned. If we "own up to" our sin, God will always forgive us. This shows God is faithful and always fair ("just"). When we confess our sins and tell God we are sorry and truly mean it, God not only forgives the sin but takes it away forever so that it is as if we had never sinned at all ("purify us from all unrighteousness").

Believe in Jesus.

> *"Believe in the Lord Jesus, and you will be saved" (Acts 16:31).*

Believing is more than knowing it with your mind. It is living it with your life. For example, if you believe that a chair will hold you up when you sit in it, you don't really believe it unless you are willing to sit in it. You must not only believe that God will forgive your sin if you ask him to, but you must trust God to do it every day.

> *"For God so loved the world that he gave his one and only Son, that whosoever believes in him shall not perish but have eternal life" (Jn. 3:16).*

Use the child's name in the verse instead of "the world" and "if (name) believes in him, she/he shall not perish" instead of "whosoever." Let the child know that if he or she had been the only person in the world who had ever sinned, God would have sent Jesus to die for him or her. Because of God's great love for every person, God sent Jesus. Any and every person who believes in him with his or her whole life will not die inside, but will go to live with God forever when his or her body dies.

Tell others about your faith in Jesus.

> *"Whoever acknowledges me before men, I will also acknowledge him before my Father in heaven" (Mt. 10:32).*

"Acknowledge" means to tell others that you know Jesus as the one that you want to follow from now on. When we are willing to tell others about our decision, then Jesus is willing to tell God, the Father, that we are God's children, too, because of Jesus.

One way that we acknowledge Jesus is to be baptized because he was baptized and we want to follow his example. It is a way to show others a picture of what we have chosen to do. We are going to follow Jesus with God's help.

Follow Jesus' way

> *"You are my friends if you do what I command" (Jn. 15:14).*

When we confess our sin and ask for forgiveness, God forgives us, but we are to be so sorry that we want to live our lives the way Jesus showed us how to live when he was on earth. To be Christ followers and Jesus' friends, we must study the Bible and learn what Jesus commanded us to be. We also need to pray and listen to what God may be telling us about the way to live our lives. When we don't make good choices, we ask God to forgive us and to help us make better choices.

Responding to God's invitation

Give the child this information if needed: "When it is time for you to make this decision, God the Holy Spirit will tell you. God will not be a voice you hear with your ears, but you will know that God wants you to confess your sins, ask for forgiveness, and decide to follow God's way of living for the rest of your life. You can't live a life that is perfect, so God will come to live inside of you and help you to live the kind of life that is pleasing to God. This is the most important decision you will ever make in your life."

Make sure that the child understands that this is a decision between him or her and God and no one else. Everyone has to make this choice for himself or herself regardless of what anyone else wants him or her to do.

These scriptures and explanations are only an outline of the dialogue you might have with a child. Let the child ask questions. Sometimes these questions may be "off track," but that is okay as long as the child gets the basic information and knows his or her role in responding to God's invitation. Every discussion will be different. Trust that the Holy Spirit will be working through you, the counselor, as well as the child during the entire process.

Follow-up strategies

When a child has made a decision to become a Christian and be a Christ follower, it is not the end of conversion. Some people breathe a sigh of relief and move on to the next child. However, salvation is only the beginning of becoming a Christ follower. A church that is concerned about the faith journey of all of its congregants will have a discipling strategy for all ages.

Discipleship in reality begins with preschoolers and grade-schoolers prior to their accepting Christ into their lives. As parents and teachers guide children through praying, learning Bible truths, singing praises, and other spiritual experiences, they are laying the groundwork for a life of following Christ.

On the other hand, after the child has declared his or her desire to live life the way God wants the child to live it rather than how he or she desires to live it, the child will benefit from learning how to grow more deeply in that relationship with God. Classes that teach the spiritual disciplines, the church ordinances, the responsibilities of being in a faith family (stewardship and service, for example), as well as how to communicate the faith to others are helpful in continuing to help the child be a growing follower.

Julie was a fortunate child to have had a family and a church prepared for this special day in her life. Their positive guidance will give her a solid start in her new relationship with Jesus Christ.

Notes

[1]Widely accepted statistic noted in Karen Stephens, "Primed for Learning: The Young Child's Mine," Beginning Workshops column, *Child Care Information Exchange* (March 1999): 45.

CHAPTER 7

Does Communication Flow among Staff, Parents, and Teachers in all Ministries, as well as in the Congregation?

The teacher in the fifth grade Sunday Bible study class had just begun a guided discussion with the children about how they could have personal relationships with Jesus Christ. The door abruptly opened, and the leader of the children's choir motioned for the children who were singing that Sunday morning in the worship service to go with her to practice in the worship center. As more than half of the class exited, the careful preparation of the conscientious teacher was destroyed. The message that the choir leader inadvertently sent this volunteer was, "What I do is more important than what you do," or perhaps, "Music performance is more important than Bible study."

Consider the volunteer who arrives at a team meeting prepared to plan an upcoming event, only to be informed by a paid staff member that in the interest of time, the decisions have been made and the volunteer needs only to implement the plans in the manner prescribed.

One Sunday, a new security system for identifying children is instituted in a church. The parents were notified in a letter that it would begin this day, but no one has told them how it works or why it is needed. The members of the congregation who do not have children hear the parents complaining about the chaos as they registered and left their children, and now they are wondering if "something" has happened to create such a "drastic measure."

Almost weekly a church will experience lack of adequate communication between

- paid staff and volunteer teachers
- teachers/leaders and parents
- teachers in one ministry and teachers in another ministry
- two or more paid clergy
- ministry teams or committees…
  and the list goes on and on.

This lack of careful, intentional communication creates much of the conflict and confusion experienced in churches. The larger the church, the more communication must be a priority.

Churches differ in the ways decisions are made as well as implemented. Some churches rely on their paid clergy/staff to initiate programming as well as to guide day-to-day decisions. Other churches use ministry teams, committees, or other coordinating groups to guide the ministry of the church. A significant number of churches use a combination of staff-led and volunteer-led decision making. It is important for everyone to know the processes by which ministries are implemented and to communicate effectively using that process.

Communication among Clergy/Church Staff and Volunteer Leaders

If a church relies on its paid clergy/staff to develop and guide its preschool and grade-school children's ministries, they must establish methods of communication with the volunteer leaders that not only inform them in a timely manner but also invite them into the process. Many forms of communication are available today. Churches, especially church staff, need to utilize all of them to appeal to the preferred style of each volunteer. Remember that the volunteers are bombarded with messages from a variety of sources, and you must find a way to capture their attention. That means that you will have to be creative and prolific because few people remember a message delivered only once. Consider these communication possibilities and vary your approaches:

- A monthly, bi-weekly, or weekly written communication that reminds and informs volunteers of upcoming events or highlights past experiences helps everyone to understand as well as prepare for their ministry commitments. Include notes about changes in the regularly scheduled programming, thus avoiding last-minute changes that can frustrate volunteers. If the newsletter or flyer is age-group specific for childhood ministry, it can include a variety of ministry-related items. Upcoming events, new procedures, leader or child commendations, teacher training tips, or gentle reminders are all appropriate for such a communiqué. The children and volunteers can contribute to it as well by sharing their learning experiences or special events, either past or present. Start promotion of major events or procedures weeks in advance if you want people to read and respond to important information and to get it included in their plans. Many people schedule and plan far ahead.
- A yearly calendar with major emphases and events given to the volunteers when they commit to the ministry will help them to make their plans to include the events or find others to serve in their place when they must be gone. Many people today need several months'

notice to schedule their commitments. Be sure to check the school and community calendars that may impact participation at the church's events. Each community has its attendance "quirks," so you must coordinate the church events to match the patterns of the congregation, or the minister/coordinator, the leadership volunteers, and the families will all express frustration.

- Reminder communications nearer the time of the event will help volunteers to know they are not only needed but also valued as important team members. Leaders and parents attempt to remember information from work, their child's school, their spouse's work, their community organizations or boards, as well as church. Last-minute announcements can remind the leader or parent who is overloaded with information.
- The forms of communication should be the ones that suit your time, resources, and style as well as the ones to which your volunteers seem to pay attention. Newsletters, information flyers, e-mail messages, skits and dramas at gathering times, and sometimes telephone messages all have good points and weaknesses. Multiple forms of the same message will be necessary for the most important information or reminders.

Volunteers also need to be in relationship with the staff, especially the one(s) who supervises their area of ministry. Face-to-face communication is extremely important in establishing relationships and cooperation. The minister/age group coordinator needs to be around when the programs or events are occurring, encouraging the leadership and reminding them of any important information. Short, monthly meetings with volunteer leadership are very beneficial in some churches.

Communication among Staff/Volunteer Leaders and Parents

Another source of conflict arises because parents are not adequately informed about what has been planned for their children or families. Last-minute information, inadequate advertising, or poor scheduling may result in poor attendance. In today's world, church events are only some of the many good options available to children and families. Events must be planned well and with excellence if we are to compete for the precious time of children and parents. If the event is worthy of their time, then parents must be given adequate notice and information to schedule their calendars for the event or perhaps make adjustments with engagements already on their calendars. We cannot expect them to make last-minute adjustments when we have not communicated in a timely fashion.

Procedures and policies regarding the ministry need to be communicated clearly and with sensitivity. Sometimes we assume parents and leaders understand the purpose of procedures and policies, but lack of understanding often leads to hurt feelings and perhaps anger. Written communication to the homes of your parents and children carries a lot of importance in today's fast-paced world. Letters, cards, newsletters, e-mails, and flyers all help to assure parents of your concern for them as well as their children. One typical mother shared that when her family was looking for a church to join, they noted which ones communicated with their child in the week following their initial visit. That personal contact carried a great deal of weight in their perception of a caring faith community.

Remember that most parents are not interested in supporting a church program. They are interested in supporting ministries that help their children to love God and love others, and they will respond with their time and commitment if we truly plan with their needs and the needs of their children in mind.

Communication among Teachers

Shared space

Almost every church must use education space for more than one organization during a given week. Good stewardship would encourage the use of the preschool and grade-school classrooms multiple times during the week for a variety of ministries. However, shared space issues are the most common conflicts between teachers/leaders that have classes or activities in the same classroom or teaching space throughout the week or month. This is especially true if one ministry occupies the room(s) many hours during the week while others may be in the room only one or two hours a week.

Ownership of "a room" often becomes the source of conflict because the adult leaders "take possession" of the teaching or activity space. A guiding principle is that the space belongs to the preschoolers or grade-schoolers that are in the room multiple times a week, not their leadership. If the room belongs to the children and not the teachers, then everyone can work together to prepare the room for the learning experiences of the children. Teachers do not "own" the room or space, so no one teacher can say "my room" no matter how many hours he or she occupies it. Guiding teachers to adopt this ownership perspective is not easy, but it will eliminate many differences once they embrace it.

Lack of communication among the teachers creates conflict that can lead to accusations, frustration, and often resignations. "They didn't…" becomes a common accusation in ministries lacking good communication between ministry leaders who are sharing space.

Some churches have discovered that an annual gathering of the leaders sharing a room helps to clarify expectations for

- room arrangement
- replenishment of expendable, shared supplies
- use of bulletin boards or wall space (perhaps designating space for each ministry)

- location/storage of ministry-specific materials
- condition of room when each ministry leaves the room

Sometimes a mid-year gathering to evaluate the shared-space agreements made earlier might be helpful or even necessary. Some teachers will be sharing well while others may need to tweak the agreement a bit. Keep the meeting positive and affirming, encouraging the teachers to keep working at it for the sake of the preschoolers and grade-schoolers who need the example of their teachers sharing as they are teaching them to do.

If some of the teachers/leaders are paid for their ministry leadership, they may need to be subject to higher expectations for adjusting furniture and equipment for the ministries led by volunteers than are the volunteers. For example, if a weekday preschool ministry meets in a room several days a week, but some of the equipment and teaching materials are not appropriate for the Bible study class on Sunday, then the weekday teachers need to be responsible for putting away the inappropriate materials on Friday and returning them on Monday.

When teachers perceive that other teachers respect their ministries, they tend to engage in less blaming and accusations and more cooperation and mutual support. This does not happen easily or quickly, but with increased communication and encouragement, even teachers in different ministries can begin to build a team spirit.

Planning

Communication among teachers/leaders in the same program and classroom is essential for children to have truly effective teaching/learning experiences. Every teacher "doing his or her own thing" is very poor teaching methodology, and what we are teaching the children is crucial to their faith formation. The ideal planning interaction is face-to-face meetings at least once a month. For example, sometimes a church will suggest a scheduled planning time for Bible study teachers to meet together. Other churches encourage teachers to gather for a planning session when it is convenient with their schedules, often before or after other scheduled church programs.

During a planning time, teachers/leaders will

- pray together for the preschoolers or children, their families, and the teaching sessions
- discuss administrative issues such as anticipated teacher absences, classroom organization and operation, bulletin boards (if you have them), needed supplies, security issues, etc.
- preview the literature (Bible study, missions, music, etc.), discuss the purpose of the session, review the content, and make preparation assignments for each teacher or leader

If you are planning in the teaching room, begin collecting the teaching materials and preparing the room unless another group will be using the room before your next session. If a face-to-face meeting is not feasible or agreeable, telephone calls and e-mail messaging are better than nothing at all. Encourage some type of planning communication, however unconventional it may be. Each teacher or leader needs to understand not only what his or her particular leadership responsibilities for the session are but also the purpose for the session. All of the teachers need to know more than a body of information. They must know what they are trying to guide the children to know and apply to their lives.

Communication of the childhood ministry with the congregation

One reason that childhood ministry is often "invisible" to the larger congregation is that we do not tell "our story" of what is happening. Parents and leadership in the ministry may know (or may not know), but other adults in the church may never encounter the ministry directly. Therefore, it is important to inform the congregation about how disciples are being made and families are being equipped in their mission.

Consider some of these story communications:

- Stories in church or childhood ministry newsletters or on a church Web page about a class experience, a child's insight, a teacher's testimony, or a parent's encouraging word of appreciation;
- Eye-catching bulletin boards or Web page ads where parents and other adults can see advertisements of upcoming events or a display celebrating an event that just occurred;
- Reports in story form at your church council, church ministry team, diaconate or elder meeting, or other churchwide planning group;
- Churchwide events in which children and their leaders have high visibility as full participants;
- Attractive brochures that summarize the preschool and grade-school ministries–make these available to all church members to give to new neighbors or others they meet who have children;
- An annual Children's Sunday during which the grade-school children are the primary worship leaders;
- A video or multimedia presentation of events held throughout the year and put into a production shown as a part of an important event at church;
- A display of projects the children have made as a part of their learning experiences–even interspersed throughout the year;
- Sharing of items that the ministry needs–books, furnishings, teaching materials, playground equipment, etc.–and encouraging of Bible study groups, missions organizations, or other small groups to participate in securing the needed items;
- Using preschool and grade-school teachers as congregational worship leadership.

Use the talents and gifts of your children and their teachers/leaders to discover other ways of informing the congregation of the good and exciting accomplishments of the preschool and grade-school children's ministry.

Communication among Paid Clergy

To avoid conflict or competition for the same time, space, or people, a church staff that is planning together must share the resources, schedule, and coordination needed among the ministries. When ministries are complementary and in harmony, leaders feel mutual support and encouragement. Such a spirit among staff communicates how other leaders can work together to accomplish the mission and vision of the church.

However, when events are planned and consideration is not given to how they will impact other areas of ministry such as childcare or parent scheduling, conflict occurs; and the church's ministry is weakened. This communication is most effectively conveyed in regularly scheduled staff meetings so that everyone can be informed and involved. In lieu of a staff meeting, you must employ other means of communication to facilitate coordination of ministries that affect the whole family. These include e-mails, telephone messages, or one-on-one meetings. The children's pastor, minister, or coordinator must be prepared to be an advocate for the children and keep their best interests before the staff as well as the church. Sometimes the children's ministry leader needs to share more than simply programming information. Sometimes you will find it necessary to share philosophical and educational information with pastors or staff that may not have experience with or understanding of preschool and grade-school ministry. The more other staff members understand what is best for the children, the better the various ministries of the church complement the needs of all of its participants.

Non-paid coordinators or directors for childhood ministry must be included in communication among the staff. All age groups must be considered in churchwide planning and programming, so periodic meetings involving paid and volunteer staff must be scheduled at a time that all can attend.

Communication to the Community

People involved in church have a tendency to think that all people know they can attend church, so if they want to, they will come. However, most people will not attend church without an invitation. The most compelling invitation comes from a person they know, but other types of communication might "invite" people to an initial encounter.

Church events advertised in the community and conducted outside are very visible to people that might drive past or walk past the church every day and not consider going inside. By encouraging people to attend a nonthreatening, even fun event, relationships can be established and attendance at other times might be considered. Some churches have used vacation Bible school, fall festivals, summer day camp, spring flings, and other family or children's events to connect with the community outside the walls of the church.

In addition, brochures, fliers, posters in community gathering places, or newsletters can target families with young children. These communications can include invitations to parenting seminars with timely topics (faith-based or general), family fun ideas, parenting tips, children's puzzles or other activities as well as an invitation to participation that includes the benefits the church can offer the children and their families.

Say It Again

When the author was involved in a new church start, the core group had no children. As young families from the community visited this church meeting in a warehouse, they decided to return after their initial visits and soon were regular attenders. Why? Because their children chose this simple little church. From parent and child accounts, the children wanted to return because of the way they were treated and taught. The parents had intended to join one of the large churches with all of the "bells and whistles" for preschoolers and grade-schoolers, but this church built relationships with the children and parents. Soon they were connected to a faith community that made a difference in their lives.

Marketing is an important secular strategy. In this world of choices, we must market our childhood ministry to the children and parents that may not first consider church as part of their options. While attractive space and engaging programming may be important in initial communication, the factor that will connect them to the childhood ministry is the relationship with people who truly care for them—both children and parents. That must be our primary communication.

CHAPTER 8

Does Your Church Offer Several Appropriate and Appealing Programs?

Every church receives a bombardment of "the latest and greatest" children's programs brochures, e-mails, and catalogs. The temptation is to pick out the one(s) that has the most appealing theme, is easiest to prepare, is most economical, offers the most "fun," or perhaps was the biggest success in a neighboring church. Some of these programs are good, but are they the best for your preschoolers and grade-schoolers and the vision you have determined for your church's ministry?

Sometimes churches become eager to "fill a time slot" when one program "isn't working," so they decide to change to create new interest. Instead of designing a balanced curriculum that is based on what the church has thoughtfully determined for its ministry, it simply implements a new program that looks interesting. Too often leaders who do not have a vision for the ministry resort to "fun" programming to attract children and families. While this might attract large numbers of children, it does not ensure that they are growing in their knowledge, faith, or experience with God. On the other hand, programs must be engaging to children so they will want to learn and experience biblical truths.

Excellent, appealing programming for preschoolers and grade-schoolers is important to parents whether they are looking for a new church or are established members. A church must provide programs that parents perceive as beneficial as well as appealing to their children. However, the childhood minister or director also must keep in mind the purpose of the program and ministry, and determine if it meets the needs of the preschoolers and grade-schoolers. Both criteria must be applied to any new programming.

Traditional Programming

Many churches still have traditional programming for preschoolers and grade-schoolers. The elements of traditional programming vary somewhat, but many of them include Bible study, discipleship, music, worship, missions or outreach, and weekday ministries such as a preschool, daycare, child development center, "Parent's Morning Out," or after-school care. These core programs usually are supplemented with dated events such as experience trips, themed parties, vacation Bible school, camps, and seasonal celebrations.

Depending on the church, these traditional programs may or may not be different from a generation ago. Some churches have exactly the same programs taught in nearly the same way as they were fifty years ago. They have little hands-on learning in activity centers with preschoolers. Grade-school children still sit around tables listening to a teacher, answering questions, or doing pencil-and-paper activities. Yet we know so much more today about how children learn best than we did fifty years ago, and the methods used in schools and the activities in which children engage at home are drastically unlike those of the previous generations.

While children are basically the same as they always have been, the world of their childhood has drastically changed, and adjustments are necessary to connect them to God and others in the most inviting ways. Some churches that understand this shift have made changes in their traditional programming so that the basic content is somewhat the same but the teaching/learning methods and environment are adjusted to meet the needs and interests of today's preschoolers and grade-schoolers.

Traditional programming in some of these "updated" churches has a new look:

Bible study

The key to excellent Bible learning for preschoolers as well as grade-schoolers is engaging them in active learning. The teacher is the most important key to a good learning session, so consistency and competency are vital (see chapter 4). In addition, teaching methods that consider the learning styles of the children are woven into each session.

Preschoolers and grade-schoolers have preferences about how they learn best. While children use all of their senses, some learn best through seeing, others through hearing, and still others through doing. Some children can learn almost anything set to music, and others like word puzzles and problem solving. Other methods that use nature, the arts, and group projects engage children with the content and its application to their lives. A good teacher will plan the lesson to meet the learning styles and interests of the children rather than the teacher's own learning preference.

A common pitfall to avoid is utilizing a method that overpowers the message or the point of the lesson. We all have watched an entertaining commercial that was memorable, but later we couldn't remember the product being advertised. An activity that is too stimulating may be a lot of fun and engage the children, but the content—which was the point of the activity—is lost in the frenzy. Finding that balance of enjoyment and learning is the goal of a good teacher and a good teaching/learning session.

A good preschool Bible study session will include most of these elements:

- Materials used or displayed in the room appear current to the lesson being taught.

- The room is arranged by activity areas or centers rather than chairs around a group of tables.
- Children have ample space in the room to move freely.
- The room does not look cluttered or "stuffed" with furniture and toys.
- The older preschoolers are allowed to choose activities at their own pace rather than everyone doing the same activity at the same time.
- The Bible is used and is accessible to preschoolers in the room or in activity centers.
- Teachers are interacting throughout the session with infants through older preschoolers.
- The younger preschoolers have a few toys/activities from which to choose rather than tubs or shelves full of toys to be strewn on the floor.
- The activities appear inviting, fresh, and safe.
- The activities allow the children to be creative and express themselves.
- The room is safe and attractive and has age-appropriate equipment, furnishings, and toys (see chapter 10).
- The teachers are prepared and ready to receive the first child who arrives.
- Three-through-five-year-olds have a short 10–15 minute group time that includes a Bible story or life application story as well as varied activities that last only 3–5 minutes each.
- Happy, busy sounds are a part of the teaching/learning experience.

A good grade-school Bible study session will include most of these elements:
- The Bible is used throughout the session by teachers and students.
- A variety of activities, methods, and materials are provided for the different learning styles of children—visual, auditory, active doing.
- Teachers sometimes relate to children individually rather than just to the group.
- Pupils are interested and involved in learning.
- Teaching is appropriate for the age and understanding of the child.
- Students are led to discover ways of applying Bible truths to their lives today.
- Children learn basic concepts on which more complex understandings may be built in years to come.
- Teachers help children discover answers and equip children to find answers by guiding their learning rather than lecturing.
- Teachers encourage children through honest praise and genuine caring.
- Children and teachers pray together.

A traditional Bible study event in a huge number of churches is still vacation Bible school or vacation church school. With historical roots that predate Sunday school, vacation Bible school has morphed from a summer-long community event in the early twentieth century to a two-week church event that reached deep into the community in the mid-twentieth century to a one-week or weekend event that is often held at night in the twenty-first century. Apparently the value of vacation Bible school is demonstrated by the churches' adjusting length, schedule, and format to accommodate the changing schedules of participants in order to keep vacation Bible school going.

Discipleship

Some Bible study sessions include elements of discipleship, but additional learning opportunities are needed for the children to learn specific discipleship knowledge, skills, and behaviors. Discipleship sessions can include the following:

- Bible skills—knowing how the Bible is organized, how to find books and passages, memorization of verses and passages appropriate for the age
- Church history stories and faith heroes
- Discovery of personal gifts and talents and their use in God's kingdom
- Responsible Christian citizenship and stewardship
- Spiritual disciplines such as prayer, Bible reading, fasting, etc.
- Conversion counseling and church membership or confirmation
- Ethical decisions and behaviors

Traditional churches often conduct children's discipleship classes when adults are having their own programming, such as a Sunday or Wednesday evening. Sometimes it is a weekly meeting, but increasingly discipleship classes are becoming short-term sessions lasting 4–6 sessions or weeks per topic.

Sadly, childhood discipleship is not a priority for most churches. Meaningful life routines and habits are begun at a young age. While children may not have yet professed their faith in Christ, becoming Christ followers has its roots even in the preschool years as they learn to pray, listen to Bible stories, find Bible thoughts with colored markers, hear the faith stories of their parents and teachers, and learn how they can take care of God's world.

By designing short discipleship units or even single lessons, some churches are using formerly church "childcare" situations as discipleship opportunities. Whenever children are in the care of church workers with purpose and materials, the occasion is ripe for discipleship teaching. Possible discipleship training could occur with children of adult choir members who are practicing, during preschool worship care, and in after-school care, for example.

Congregations who want to grow their children to become obedient Christ followers will plan intentional discipleship programming that includes knowledge and experiences to connect children with God and to the church God loves so much.

Missions and outreach

When Jesus left this earth, he left all of us who follow him with the instructions to "go and make disciples of all nations" (Mt. 28:19a). Whether a church calls that missions, outreach, or another term, it involves both teaching our children about how the church tells others about Jesus and involving them in mission actions as they are capable. Mission education in traditional churches often includes stories of missionaries and the people groups to whom they minister. Stories of missionaries overseas involve cultural exposure when teachers introduce foods, clothing, and other hands-on experiences that are different from ones with which the children are familiar. Missionaries who serve people in our own country who are culturally the same or different can open children to the possibility of their own involvement in missions.

Mission actions expose children to how they can be missionaries, too. Every community has mission needs that children can address, including food banks, clothes closets, or food packets to hand to people asking for food on street corners. Your local judicatory or social service agency could identify those to which your children might respond. Before getting children involved, you will need to contact the people and agencies involved and determine needs your group can meet.

Some churches separate their grade-school children into boy and girl mission groups, but increasing numbers are mixing the genders while dividing them into age groups. Both types of groupings have advantages. The availability of adequate, committed leadership, the behavior of the children, and the purpose of the program will guide a church to adopt one or the other.

Music

Preschool and grade-school music groups unfortunately are frequently viewed as performance preparation groups or choirs. A better point of view sees them as a way to encourage children to worship God through the expressive path of music. Perhaps we have lost the enjoyment of singing, clapping, and dancing our praise to God as the people in the Old Testament modeled for us (Ps. 98:4–6; Ex. 15:20). We view the children as performers for us rather than for God.

Churches that are most effective in their music programs incorporate music appreciation, age-appropriate concepts of music theory, movement, listening, as well as singing in their classes. Music is experienced in all of its various expressions by the preschoolers and grade-schoolers. One church is known in the community for its excellent and holistic music program that meets each week after school. Grade-schoolers from this small town go to this church to learn, worship, and participate in musical experiences. Some of the children are not involved in any other programs of the church and thus hear the gospel through the music of this ministry.

Many traditional churches also have grade-school children's handbell and chime groups and interpretive dance groups. They also use the talents of individuals who play various instruments well. All of these groups or individuals can be used for worship service participation, but emphasis should be on their musical praise and offering to God, not performance for the church.

Worship

Worship with preschoolers and grade-schoolers was discussed in chapter 2. The point to make here is that preschoolers and grade-schoolers need to have worship education as a part of the church programming. At whatever age preschoolers or grade-schoolers enter the congregational worship experience, they (and perhaps the parents guiding them) need a worship education class to orient them to the meaning of the various parts of the worship service so they can derive the most possible meaning from the worship experience.

If they were a part of a children's church (worship service), and its purpose was to integrate the children meaningfully into the congregational worship experience, then perhaps a special welcome and a reminder requesting patience from the congregation will allow the children to acclimate to the new worship format.

Weekday ministries

The traditional weekday ministries most often include a half-day preschool program, a full-day childcare or child development center, a before- and/or after-school care program, a Mother's Morning Out (sometimes called Parent's Morning Out), or Mothers of Preschoolers (MOPS). These programs provide a ministry for the community as well as for the church members.

A church considering starting one of these weekday ministries would be wise to survey the community to determine which weekday ministry is most needed. A large downtown city church, thinking about starting a full-day childcare center, surveyed the people in the nearby buildings and discovered that they preferred to leave their children in neighborhood childcare centers rather than bring the children into the city. In other situations churches have discovered a need for a half-day program or a Parent's Morning Out because the community has many stay-at-home moms and other full-day childcare centers are servicing the working parents.

The goals for a weekday ministry are to provide a safe and nurturing place for children, to meet the needs of parents and children with quality care in a Christian environment, and to guide the spiritual, physical, mental, emotional, and social development of each child. To reach its full potential, weekday ministry in any form must have the total support of the entire church.

A church weekday ministry has a special opportunity to integrate faith into the total childcare experience. Unlike secular programs, the teachers, the curriculum, and the materials can be appropriate in all areas of the child's development, even faith formation. The ministry needs to be forthcoming about its intention to nurture faith, and never be apologetic for its purpose. In addition to faith formation, the curriculum must include a balance of good physical, emotional, social, and mental developmentally appropriate practices. This curriculum should not push preschoolers, but instead enrich and expand their experiences so that they are prepared for the academic world of school.

Grade-school ministries need to have a curriculum that considers all areas of human development rather than offering a childcare program that has no purpose other than to keep the children safe and encourage them to do their homework. A rich curriculum that includes cooperative recreation, purposeful games with opportunities for teamwork, special interest activities (art, music, nature, etc.), special tutoring, as well as biblical and application stories, discussions, and learning activities will be stimulating and substantive for grade-school children.

A weekday program must never have the purpose of "making money" for the church. Instead, a quality program that has the best interests of the children and parents in mind will require some financial resources from the church, especially in the first few years. The church will need to decide that the weekday program is a ministry of the church worthy of financial support. At the same time, the church should expect and encourage good financial practices by the ministry.

A Church Weekday Education Committee or Board is important in helping a ministry to stay connected with and integrated into the overall church vision. They will be the support system and governing body for the ministry and the director. Include people who have a passion for the ministry, some who have some business and/or human resources experience, parents, teachers in other preschool or grade-school church ministries, the director of the program, and the staff member who has supervisory responsibilities. Regular meetings will ensure that the ministry will stay an integral part of the total preschool and grade-school children's ministry.

Creative Programming

Some churches have ventured into programming that is a bit "outside the box" in an attempt to connect with a changing childhood and world. "Innovative" or "contemporary" churches are willing to try something new that they have reason to believe will work better in their context than a traditional approach. Even some otherwise traditional churches are trying some creative preschool and grade-school children's programming to attract families who are not attending church at all.

Bible study/discipleship

Churches that do not have traditional "Sunday school" often use the *worship service time* to have Bible study and/or discipleship with the preschoolers and/or grade-school children. Many of these churches still have age-graded groupings, but some have the grade-schoolers in a large group part of the time with dramas, lively music, puppets, and computer generated graphics. Then they divide them into small groups, each with an adult leader. Churches that do not have the grade-school children in a worship experience need to consider how these children will learn to worship. Worship is something that does not just happen; it requires experience, instruction, and exposure to worshiping role models.[1] The "window of opportunity" is around 7–9 years of age, when children often "adopt" the beliefs of those people who are most important to them.[2] Inclusion in the worshiping community as a full participant rather than as a patient observer is an important programming consideration for all churches.

Other churches use a *rotation system,* with a group of children experiencing the same story each week using a different method or learning style. As stated earlier in chapter 4, some cautions need to be considered with rotation teaching. It is a convenience for adults, but not the most effective system for children whose faith is rooted in relationship.

Churches that have *small group Bible study/fellowship* during the week need to recognize the potential of this time with the children of the adult participants. The preschoolers and grade-schoolers can benefit from this weekly gathering as well, and leaders from other small groups can teach the children without adults having to miss their own group experiences. Discipleship content is especially suited to this time, especially learning Bible skills through games. Extending learning from Sunday's Bible lesson or dialogue around application of the Bible truths are other options.

Even some traditional churches that have limited programming time have begun integrating discipleship into the Bible study period. Conversion counseling or confirmation classes sometimes are formed as a temporary special grouping during Sunday school. Other units on church history and beliefs as well as spiritual disciplines and Bible skills are sprinkled in throughout the year, sometimes integrated into the Bible study material and sometimes as a stand-alone unit.

Intergenerational (or multigenerational) Bible study is another creative approach some churches have found enriching to the church and its families. One church has groups that meet every Sunday morning for three months in homes not far from the church during the church Bible study hour. About eight to ten families with preschoolers and/or grade-schoolers and teens gather for a common Bible story, lesson, or verse based on a theme.

Then they have "together activities" and sometimes separate age-graded activities that are shared with the whole group at the end of the session. During the rest of the year, the families join the regular age-graded Bible study program of the church.

Summer is a good time to try intergenerational Bible study, even during "Sunday school." A church can group using biological families, or create multigenerational "families." Children need to hear the faith stories of seasoned Christians that they know and admire. Adults need to hear the thoughts and fresh perspectives of children and teens who have just begun their faith journey. We have much to remember and learn from each age, and this is a rich format for sacred stories and experiences springing from relationships.

Modern *vacation Bible school* has creative expressions. Working mothers and fathers, year-round school schedules, and the plethora of summer options have driven some churches to become creative in schedules and formats to keep VBS as a significant church event. Weekend Bible schools that meet Friday evening, Saturday morning and early afternoon, Sunday morning and afternoon, and end late Sunday afternoon with a celebration are becoming increasingly popular, although they cannot have as many learning experiences as those that meet every morning or night for a week.

Some churches have vacation Bible school in the morning and day camp in the afternoon, thus appealing to those families needing full-day care for their children. One large suburban church has two weeks of VBS, one week in the morning and one week later in the summer at night, using two different groups of teachers. This format accommodates the stay-at-home moms and dads as well as the dual-career parents.

Still other churches have vacation Bible schools outside in neighborhoods or multihousing complexes, and a few churches have VBS during non-summer breaks such as spring break or year-round school breaks. VBS is very flexible and now has many expressions, adjusting to the community and church participation patterns.

Missions/music

With families choosing to give less of their time to church programming, congregations are trying some creative combinations. A few churches that value both music and missions programs, but find it increasingly difficult to engage families for two additional hours each week, are combining the two. While several churches are simply cutting down the time for each to a half hour, others are designing an integrated music and missions curriculum. At this point they are designing their own literature and using teachers with strengths in music and/or missions.

Other churches are implementing creative missions approaches. One church decided that to "raise up" adults with Christ's heart for missions and service, they needed to let their children have hands-on experiences so that service to others would become a lifestyle and not just a "someday, sometime" occurrence. They changed their day camp purpose from the children being on the receiving end of trips and fun activities to being the deliverers of joy, hope, and help to others. While they continued to have recreation and a creative learning time about the missions need for the week, their focus was on helping others. Teens served as junior counselors, so they were involved in doing missions as well.

The first and second graders helped prepare the week's missions materials, and the third through fifth graders did some preparation but mainly delivered the service. They planted border plants down the sidewalk of a house used as a homeless shelter, bought prizes and played Bingo with nursing home residents, painted and sorted donated items at a women's shelter, purchased and dressed teddy bears for a patrolman's intervention program, and engaged in many other discovered needs in the community.

Multigenerational experiences

Families are spending less time together than in previous generations, and church age-grading only adds to the time apart. Intergenerational activities provide time for families and/or church families of several generations to interact and connect while learning about each other's stories and faith journeys.

In addition to the multigenerational Bible studies mentioned earlier, some churches are including more multigenerational activities in their programming. Seasonal activities during Advent, Thanksgiving, and Lent are optimum times. In addition, other gatherings have become more inclusive of many ages—family retreats or camping experiences, multi-age choirs, intergenerational vacation Bible schools, and other special events designed with multiple ages in mind.

Sixth-grade pre-teen ministry

Sixth grade middle schoolers are like no other age. They are sometimes children and sometimes adolescents. Because of their "betwixt-and-between" age, they benefit greatly from a special ministry. Yet in many churches, sixth graders are in the same programs as high school teens. Churches that want to minister to the needs of this vulnerable age will want to rethink their strategy and consider a sixth grade ministry that will prepare these children for the turbulent teenage years rather than throwing them into the middle of teenage angst.

One church has enlisted a team of adults who are passionate about this age and the potential for preparing them for the turbulent teens. This team of eight people rotates primary responsibilities for each of the sixth grade programs, but all of them are present for most of the activities. They also conduct special events throughout the year in which only sixth graders can participate. Not even the youth ministry includes the specific events reserved for that sixth grade year. While this is a medium-sized church, other smaller churches have as few as five to seven sixth graders in a pre-teen Sunday Bible study ministry. Even that special attention in one church program is proving helpful to the faith and social/emotional needs of pre-teens in many churches.

Program Development Process

Often churches implement a new program without using a process that could ensure its success even before it is begun. For many years Dr. Brian Lee, senior pastor of Lafayette Baptist Church in Fayetteville, North Carolina, has used a process that has also proven successful in many other churches. The *Program Development Process*[3] has "filters" or questions that must be answered affirmatively before implementing the program. If a negative response occurs at any point, the process is stopped, and the program is not implemented.

When a program is first conceived, the initial filter is the *Purpose Filter*. To determine its purpose, a ministry would ask such questions as whether this program accomplishes the vision of the ministry, would explore whether it is the most effective way to accomplish the vision, and would establish whether this program would help the congregation accomplish its overall mission and vision.

Next would be the *Need Filter*. Determine if this program avoids duplication of other ministries. Consider if adding this program would maintain the balance of your ministry or make it too heavy in one area, such as Bible study, discipleship, worship, etc. Would it take the place of another program or be an addition? If it is taking the place of another program, is it meeting the need that the other program met, or would a need go unmet with the change? The ministry infrastructure needs to be evaluated to see if sufficient budget resources, church space, and calendar space are available for the new program.

In addition, the *Need Filter* includes defining who cares about this or has a need for it. Sometimes the adults or parents have a need the preschoolers or grade-schoolers do not have. First and foremost, if it is a childhood ministry program, it must meet a need of the children.

The *Theological Filter* reminds us to check the theology of the program to determine if it matches the theology of the church and ministry. While some programs are appropriate in one church, they would be inconsistent with the teachings of another. It is important that the theological content be considered before it is implemented. Would this program clearly communicate to those outside the church what your church believes?

An extremely crucial filter for preschool and grade-school ministry is the *Leadership Filter*. First, do you have gifted leaders who are passionate about this program and who are not already "loaded" with other responsibilities? Do they have the right personalities for this program? Are they trained to do it? Leaders would need to know what the expectations are for this assignment and whether a support system is in place to help them be successful.

If the program has cleared all of these filters with affirmative answers, the next filter is the *Logistics Filter.* The age group minister needs to determine if the church staff is fully supportive of this program, as well as the church coordinating group that offers its support in most churches. Then it is appropriate to verify the funding and the starting date and time that is officially on the planning calendar. A suitable location for the ministry and the necessary literature and supplies must be secured. Substantial advertising will inform people that something new is about to happen in which they will want to participate. Other logistical items may need attention, depending on the type of program.

Before the program is implemented, consider *Evaluation Filter 1,* which is a date on which the program will be evaluated based on criteria that will define success for this program. Even before implementing the program, you need to outline an exit strategy should the program not be successful.

The last filter, *Evaluation Filter 2,* occurs on the date established in *Evaluation Filter 1.* At this time the church and/or childhood minister will determine if a program is successful based on the established criteria. Does the program need to continue? Are there improvements that need to be made to the program to make it stronger? Should the church admit the program has not met expectations and needs to be replaced or discontinued? If a church will be this intentional in planning new programs from conception to implementation, it will enjoy more successful, effective programs and suffer less chaos from poor planning.

Notes

[1]Shirley Morgenthaler, *Exploring Children's Spiritual Formation: Foundational Issues* (River Forest, Ill.: Pillars Press, 1999).

[2]John H. Westerhoff III, *Will Our Children Have Faith?,* rev. ed. (Harrisburg, Pa.: Morehouse, 2000), 91ff.

[3]Brian Lee, senior pastor of Lafayette Baptist Church in Fayetteville, N.C., includes this process in a course at Campbell University Divinity School and granted permission for its mention in this book.

CHAPTER 9

Is There a Balance between Reaching New Children and Families and Nurturing Those Already Involved?

A couple of decades ago, the author helped to start a new church. We were very eager to cultivate relationships with people who visited our services, programs, and activities. When we built our first church building in a brand new housing development, we were proactive in going door-to-door, having outdoor events to which we invited everyone in the community, and conducting children's activities in yards of members in the neighborhood.

We grew in number quickly and soon built our second building. It seemed we didn't have to work very hard at getting new participants anymore. Our attention focused on planning programs for the abundance of children attending our church already. Even the weekday preschool always had capacity enrollment and a waiting list without any effort on our part. It became difficult to get anyone to contact or especially visit guests who had attended our services, and outreach into the community to invite unchurched people disappeared. Our planned programs were full, and we were comfortable with our perceived success!

The Case for Ministry to Children "In" and "Out" of Church

The problem with this "success" was that the church was out of balance. The children in attendance were getting excellent ministry while they were at church, and we focused all of our energy on that task. However, we had lost sight of the hundreds of children and families even within a three-mile radius whose spiritual nurturing seemed to be "none of our concern." Also within that three-mile radius was a low income, ethnically diverse community with many needs that we and our resources could have addressed if we had been willing.

Some of Jesus' last words to his followers were to "be my witnesses," and to start in "Jerusalem," the city where they were (Acts 1:8). While they witnessed as they went, they continued to go "to the ends of the earth." Those are our instructions as Christ followers today, too. Many ministers, directors, or even laypersons cannot name even one child who is not involved in any church except perhaps for a child or two who have visited a church program or ministry of their church. Often if they can name one or two children, they are concerned about how the children are participating in the church programs rather than how the church can minister to their needs whatever they are.

The opposite of a church like the one described above is the congregation that expends money and energy on bus or van ministries to bring the preschoolers and grade-schoolers to the church, but once they are there, do not have quality ministries that address those children's unique needs *as well as* the needs of children "brought up in the church." Simply "going" is not enough because we are also instructed to "make disciples" (Mt. 28:19). Just because a child is in church does not mean we are making disciples. At best it is a "hit or miss" proposition unless the church understands the needs of the children and how the church could best meet those needs.

The worst scenario is when children are brought to the church, the parents of the children already attending do not want their children around "those children," and, in some churches, completely separate programs and worship services are planned for the "church children" and the "bus ministry children." Tragically, little attention is given to reaching the parents of the children brought to the church. That would be the greatest ministry a church could provide for a child—hopefully resulting in Christian parents who would be guiding them daily into relationship with Christ.

Sometimes the ministry to the unchurched is most effective if it is accomplished outside of the church building or, in some cases, begun outside and perhaps brought inside at some later point. Getting the children in the church building is not the point—attending to their spiritual as well as physical, mental, emotional, and social needs is the purpose of such a ministry. The church will need to evaluate the best location for reaching the most preschoolers and grade-schoolers and meeting their needs in the most successful way. Often community centers are looking for groups to provide programming. Even attending to the physical needs of homes, yards, and people can open doors to relationships that can develop into lasting connections.[1] The church willing to give attention to the preschoolers, grade-schoolers, and families already in church as well as those not yet attending any church must work at balancing "going" and "making disciples." That missional perspective will involve having a strategy for meeting the needs of a variety of children and families.

Reaching the Unchurched Child and Family for Church Programs

Children whose parents have not engaged them in church experiences from a young age and who have not been taught "appropriate church behavior" will need some guidance and instruction. While churches have a range of acceptable behaviors, depending on the style of the church, every congregation needs to have established behavioral guidelines so that children know where the boundaries are and how they can function optimally. If the behavioral expectations are not realistic based on development—for example, expecting a toddler to sit still for thirty minutes without wiggling—then the experience will not be the most advantageous for the child or the leaders.

Next, the teachers/leaders need to have training in guiding preschoolers and grade-schoolers who have not been in church regularly. They will need to learn how to discipline by guiding behavior rather than by punishing. Being consistent, calm, firm, and kind is the most effective discipline approach. Keeping the teacher-pupil ratios even lower than usually recommended will help with children who need more individual guidance until they adjust to the routine and expectations.

Preschoolers will need to learn that they may not hit anyone, throw anything, bite another child, or grab toys away from others. The most effective method with older preschoolers as well as grade-schoolers is called disciplinary consequences. A child is told after an incident that if they choose to engage in a certain behavior, they also choose the consequence that is related to the action. For example, if they choose to mark on the table with the markers, they choose to not draw with the markers for the rest of the day, or if they choose to hit another child, they choose to sit away from the other children who are playing. This method teaches them to consider the consequences *they are choosing* before they act. Consistency in enforcing the consequence is vital.

Creative teaching methods will be very important in teaching previously unchurched children. Attention spans will be short, and the activity level will be high. Channeling their energy and attention into productive/engaging learning experiences will be a challenge, but will produce success.

Children who have not grown up in the church or in a family with faith practices will not know basic Bible stories and verses. They may not be acquainted with basic concepts such as what the Bible is or how to locate books and verses, what prayer is and how to pray, who Jesus is and about his life and ministry, or what God's commandments are that guide our living. Their language will be what they have learned at home or in the neighborhood, and their social ability may consist of mostly street smarts or survival skills. Teachers and ministers must begin where the children are and patiently teach them new words, new social skills, and new concepts about God and Jesus that are not culturally based but relationship based.

The unchurched preschoolers and grade-schoolers have families who need ministry as well. Although the parents initially may not be as receptive as the children, we have a responsibility to nurture relationships with them so that the child may eventually have a home that practices love for God and others. Most parents respond to people who love and care for their children. Visits to the home, calls telling how the child is growing, and cards expressing appreciation for their children often catch the attention of a parent.

A church in a university town discovered that many of their weekday preschool parents did not attend any church. They started an adult Sunday school class just for those parents and during the first year had 15–20 parents each week doing Bible study and building relationships. Unchurched people often feel like "an outsider" in a regular Sunday school class in which members assume everyone knows what they know about the Bible and basic doctrines. A special effort must be made to build relationships with a target group class rather than simply operating side-by-side in separate classes. Fellowship times before class, or breakfasts or luncheons from time to time, might be needed to build relationships.

Reaching the Unchurched Child and Family Outside the Church Walls

Among all the appealing options the world offers, the church faces an increasing challenge to attract people who are not a part of the church culture. However, since the church is not contained in a building, we can "be the church" wherever we are. Attempting to bring the children to the church building may not be the best approach.

All Christians have daily opportunities to be the church wherever we are. As Christ's presence in the world, we can love God and others in each opportunity of our lives. Being in tune with the needs around us, listening to the hopes and hurts of others, and being "light and salt" is what Christ has called us to do. Church buildings are where we go to worship Almighty God and to become equipped to be the church in the world. We are the church as we love God and others throughout our lives.

A church that truly wants to make a difference in the lives of children and their families will need to assess the hopes and hurts of its "church field" and determine which ones it can address, whether this means increasing numbers coming to the church building or not. Not every church needs to do every ministry identified, but a church will need to determine through prayer and deliberation which ones it has the resources, passion, and committed leaders to do effectively.

After the ministries have been determined, locations in the community must be identified and permission secured from the private property owner or public facility manager. Safety and security concerns must also be addressed to protect the children, the leaders, and the church (see chapter 10). If your program is to be faith-based, make that clear as a matter of integrity. If it is to be non-faith specific as you are developing relationships, but will be faith-based at some point, make that known as well since some properties have policies and laws that govern faith-based activities. You will want to be law-abiding and have the highest integrity as a part of your witness.

The teachers or leaders will need to have training that may be particular to the type of ministry or general training in child development, creative teaching methods, discipline techniques, and first aid and emergency procedures, to name only a few possibilities. Ministries can be done weekly, monthly, or on another dependable schedule.

Churches that have become intentional about appealing to the unchurched culture are becoming more creative in their approaches. Here is a sampling of the methods various churches have designed to share the good news with preschoolers, grade-schoolers and/or families in their church community:

- One church partnered with a school to teach positive discipline techniques to parents. The pastor and childhood minister led the sessions at the school. Follow-up sessions on parenting were continued at the church.
- A small-town church implemented a tutoring program in partnership with a school that needed help with grade-schoolers who were falling behind because of language skills or learning disabilities. They purchased a house, equipped it with computers, and staffed it with trained people committed to building relationships with the children and their families.
- A church scheduled and hosted a medical/dental van from the denomination's men's missions group to provide free dental exams for preschoolers and grade-schoolers whose families could not afford dental checkups.
- A suburban church organized neighborhood gatherings that began with building relationships with parents and sharing life stories and challenges. From those discussions emerged a book study, a Bible study, and topical studies such as on parenting. These Christ followers intentionally listened with concerned hearts and shared their faith as the discussions and relationships evolved naturally.
- Summer is a popular time for many churches to hold neighborhood events. Some are held in yards where the children are invited to participate in Bible clubs, games, or crafts. Others use community centers or parks for recreation, puppet shows, or music events.
- Some churches have targeted ethnic or language groups that do not have a faith-based congregation in their language. Some of these groups have developed into mission churches and eventually into self-supporting language churches.

As you establish relationships with preschoolers, grade-schoolers, and their families through these various ministries, opportunities will appear for you to share your faith as well as to introduce the children to other people of faith. In turn, be open to God speaking to you through them as they share from another life perspective. Be genuinely involved in the lives of the children and their parents, and God will open doors you perhaps might not have known existed.

Ministry to Children and Their Families Who Attend Church

Being the daughter of a minister, the author was seldom the recipient of ministry from my childhood teachers. After all, I seldom missed any activity at church, and I enjoyed good health. My teachers simply expected me to be at church, but it would have been very encouraging if one of them had told me how much they appreciated my regular attendance and interested involvement (even if I didn't have much choice in the matter).

Preschoolers and grade-schoolers involved in the church need ministry from their teachers and leaders as well as their ministers or directors. Regular communication with regular as well as irregular attenders is encouraging and motivating. Ministry is more than a get-well wish or a "we-miss-you" card. It means letting every child know that they matter, that they are important.

Sometimes when "Everyone" is responsible for something, "Everyone" assumes "Someone Else" is doing it. Therefore, let's consider who is responsible for care ministry to the children. First of all, the minister or the director of the ministry guides the ministry to individual children. Sometimes he or she performs direct ministry, especially in times of crisis. However, he or she is not responsible for the entire care ministry to the children.

Every program in which the preschooler or grade-schooler participates needs to have a strategy for contacting the children who are involved. Perhaps one leader in each program does all of the ministry contacts, or perhaps each teacher or leader has a group of children for whom he or she is responsible. The children need to know that

- some people at church care profoundly about them;
- they are missed when they are absent for whatever reason;
- their presence blesses the lives of the teachers and other children;
- their positive contributions add benefit to the lives of the children and teachers;
- they are supported and comforted by their teachers when sad or traumatic events occur;
- they have teachers who want to celebrate the happy events in their lives.

Letting children know how much you care for them is just as important as preparing to teach them. You need to be attentive to the students while you are teaching. Making contact with them between the sessions lets the children and their parents know you truly are interested in their lives. How we communicate our interest in them can be as simple or as creative as you want to make it. The age and personality of the child will make a difference as well.

Learn the preschoolers' and grade-schoolers' names as quickly as possible. Call them by name when you see them, whether it is in class or other times you might see them at church or in the community. Find out what preschoolers like to play with most. Pay attention to their development in coordination, socialization, and attention span. Make it a priority to get to know each grade-schooler's interests, such as his or her favorite school subject, game, toy, television show, and book. What does the child collect? What sports does he play? What lessons does she take? Each preschooler and grade-schooler will be very unique, and the way we relate to each one needs to take his or her distinctive personalities and interests into consideration.

Preschoolers and grade-schoolers love to get personal mail. A picture postcard, a card with a poem, a coded message, or a simple printed note for a special occasion or no occasion at all is long remembered. A letter cut into puzzle pieces and placed in an envelope, or an activity from the last teaching session is great fun for a child. An e-mail message sent to the child is easy and inexpensive, but makes the child feel very special that a teacher would send him or her a message. Birthday and holiday greetings are natural opportunities, but consider other times "just because."

Telephone calls are a bit more difficult with preschoolers and grade-schoolers, but they also give the teacher an opportunity to connect with the child and perhaps a parent as well. Since most children are not big conversationalists on the telephone, a simple conversation is often quite sufficient. You might tell the children what they can anticipate for the next class (using a riddle or a "teaser"), what you appreciated from them or their learning in the last session, or you can catch up on games, recitals, trips, or other life events of which you are aware.

Visits to the preschoolers' or grade-schoolers' homes are incredibly beneficial. With the busy schedules of teachers and families, we need to make appointments and keep the visits a very short twenty minutes or so. Older children can be interviewed and their answers recorded in a notebook. Ask questions that would help you to learn about the interests of the child when he or she plays or goes to school. Ask the parents to fill in any information the child may not have remembered, as well as any issues of which you need to be aware as the child's teacher. Sometimes a visit to the child's room can provide much information, but be sensitive to the parents' comfort level with such a foray into their most personal living space.

At certain times, care ministry takes on special significance. When a crisis occurs in a child's life, his or her "support system" needs to respond. Teachers need not shy away from contacting the child or even being with the child even if they do not know what to say or do. Just your presence and a hug are meaningful to a child (or anyone else).

A crisis to a child may be the death of a pet, not passing to the next grade, learning that he or she or a friend are moving away, or other kinds of loss that may seem small to us but paramount to a child. Other family crises sometimes draw support for the parents, but the children need encouragement as well. The death of a grandparent, parent, sibling, or friend may be the child's first encounter with death of a special person in his or her life. Acknowledging that the child has suffered a profound loss is extremely meaningful to the child and parents, especially when it comes from teacher(s) or minister.

Building Relationships among Children

While some churches serve specific geographic neighborhoods where the children who attend know each other from school or play, our mobile American society has produced large numbers of churches that draw from a wide geographic area. Children often attend churches where they are in programs with children who do not attend their preschool or school or live in their neighborhood. Thus, they have little social time to build relationships with each other even if they are regular attenders. When a child visits a church program, he or she initially may not know even one child or teacher.

Ministry leaders must be intentional in building relationships among the children who attend as well as find ways to connect the first-time visitor to one or more children. In addition, when children who go to church and children who do not go to church build relationships, bonds that can make a difference in all of their lives are formed.

While the primary purpose of regularly scheduled church programs should not be social interaction, attention must be paid to building relationships within the teaching experience. Preschoolers can learn each other's names using a song or a game. Preschoolers who seem to get along very well together can be encouraged to sit near each other at group time or play together in the same activity area. The teacher of older preschoolers can enlist a "friend" for a new or visiting child. Some preschoolers are better at this than others, so choose a child who is sensitive and outgoing to pair with the visitor for activities and/or group time.

With grade-schoolers, learning games that have cooperative goals rather than competitive goals, group learning projects that utilize the strengths of each child, and short sharing sessions can foster relationships. Engaging the children in contacting absent children with a card or call will help them to pay attention to friends that may need encouragement. The grade-school child who is outgoing and confident will be the kind of child to enlist as a "buddy" for a visitor. Their responsibility would be to assist the guest in knowing what to do, a fear of many children in a strange environment.

Engaging the grade-schoolers in programming designed to reach the unchurched child is another way to invite them into relationships that they might not ordinarily create. They can be "assistants" to the leaders as well as participants. To do so they must understand that the programming is for the child who is not familiar with some of the things they might know about God, Jesus, the Bible, prayer, etc. The "assistants" must be ready to encourage, not "show up" the other children. Clarifying their role in the event will be important so that they will be ambassadors rather than saboteurs. Hopefully, this guidance will encourage them to form other relationships and share the good news with others in their sphere of influence.

The grade-school child will need opportunities outside the church programming time to make good friends. Ministry leaders may need to drop a suggestion to parents that they invite church friends over to play with their children. Even teachers could invite small groups of boys and girls to their houses for a meal and some games during which the children could get to know each other, though the teacher should make sure that a parent or two are a part of the activity. A "sleep-over" with boys one time and girls another could be a friend-making activity for grade-schoolers, as long as two or more nonrelated adults (most likely parents) are supervising the activity along with the teacher. Chapter 10 goes into detail further about the necessity for strict policies regarding adults' interaction with children. Because the church loves children, its policies should as much as possible ensure that no harm comes to them. The church is finally realizing that long-time church attendance or service does not preclude the teacher's being dangerous to children, as sad a reality as that is.

In addition to building relationships during ongoing programs, the church needs to sponsor non-program, "just plain fun" activities for the older preschoolers and grade-schoolers. Older preschoolers need only two-to-three planned, special activities a year while grade-school children may need six to seven activities a year. These activities can be sponsored by a program such as Sunday school or music groups, or it may be conducted by people who are willing to make a short-term commitment for one activity rather than a year-long teaching assignment. Even then, teachers of the preschoolers or grade-schoolers should be encouraged to attend and participate to expand their relationships with the children and parents.

Adapting a concept developed by Richard Ross[2] for youth ministry called "Lead Teams," the preschool and/or grade-schoolers' ministry leadership team(s) could identify potential dates and possible activities and invite teams of parents, teachers, and other interested adults to develop and conduct the special activities (see chapter 12). Some of these activities can be for the children who attend church. Others can be designed to reach new children in targeted areas. Holiday events such as Christmas, Easter, Valentine's Day, or Thanksgiving are popular, but seasonal events such as summer water experiences, spring picnics, fall carnivals, and winter "indoor" celebrations need to be considered at times that might not be as busy as a holiday occasion. Generic events such as a "Pet Parade" or a "Teddy Bear Pajama Party" for preschoolers, or a "Backwards Party" or "Bible Lands Party" would be fun anytime of the year. The key to this balance is making sure that the focus is both inside (discipling) and outside (going) the church walls. Children everywhere need to learn to love God and love others, and so do their parents.

Notes

[1]David W. Crocker, *Operation Inasmuch* (St. Louis: Lake Hickory Resources, 2005).

[2]Richard Ross, *Planning Youth Ministry: From Boot Up to Exit,* is a multimedia kit that includes video and computer resources for youth ministry.

CHAPTER 10

Is Your Church a Safe, Nurturing, Welcoming Place for Preschoolers and Grade-schoolers?

The parents arrived for the "early service." I could tell they were visitors. It was too early even for the assigned greeters to be in place, but I warmly greeted the parents and their three-year-old daughter. After securing basic information, I escorted them to the preschool room, where a teacher was present and ready for the preschool worship care experience. As the child slowly entered the room and became engaged with the teacher, I noted the parents' closely scrutinizing the room's appearance and teaching materials as well as the feeling that the teacher conveyed. Another teacher soon arrived, and the child became engaged with other arriving preschoolers in the learning activities for the morning. Satisfied that everything was fine, the parents proceeded to the worship center, and I was reminded of the importance of that first impression.

First Impression of Your Church's Ministry

Whether parents are looking for a new church or perhaps are exploring the church experience for the first time, they are looking for quality experiences for their children. Their first impression of a church is usually visual, especially the space in which childhood ministry takes place, since they situate their preschoolers and/or grade-schoolers in their classes even before going to the worship center or an adult program. Close behind the visual impression is the feeling of whether their children are in a safe and secure environment. Some indicators influence that first impression.

When families enter the church building, can they easily tell where to take their children?

Even from the outside of the building, parents need to be able to locate the closest entrance to the preschool or grade-school rooms. Signs on the buildings or designated parking spaces for parents of preschoolers are most helpful and inviting, especially for parents carrying several items, including one or more children.

Near the main entrance to the childhood education halls and in clear sight, a reception or welcome desk can provide helpful, friendly people to register the child, get parent information, provide a security tag, and guide the parents and children to their rooms. The welcome desk needs to be well-staffed with people who are familiar with the registration process and who have good people skills. The reception area needs to be as uncongested and as organized as possible, even though it will be busy.

If there is no clear entrance to the childhood area, a general church reception desk for guests needs to have an organized and informed process of registering the families and taking them to their proper rooms. If the teachers in the preschool rooms administer the security system, all registration information needs to be taken to the teacher, since he or she will be busy welcoming the preschooler to the room and giving the parents security items.

The message the church wants to send from the time a new family enters the parking lot is that they are valued and important to the church—and to God!

As they go down the hallways of the church, what do they experience?

The hallways in preschoolers' and grade-schoolers' space need to be inviting—bright and clean with uncluttered walls and floors. Wide hallways that do not feel like a "traffic jam" of parents and children are especially appealing. People without children should have optional access halls to their rooms and worship center to avoid congestion and possible safety issues.

Large murals down a hallway may be interesting to parents but often prove overwhelming and even frightening from the perspective of a small child. Churches sometimes decorate hallways with framed pictures. Pictures that are hung only at adult eye-level and appeal to adults, rather than low-hung pictures designed for children, send the message that this space is for adults instead of children. While the parents may be personally impressed, their children will not be; and they often have the final "vote." Pictures that are of interest to children and hung at their eye-level (and perhaps changed from time to time) offer continuous interest to children who must look at knees most of the time!

At the same time, the hallways do not need to be cluttered with whimsical paraphernalia that implies it is more of a theme park than a delightful place to learn about God. Fantasy or cartoon figures may make an impressive initial appeal but lose their attraction after a few weeks. Children don't go to a theme park every week. A more child-inviting hallway over weeks of navigation will be free of clutter, have colorful but not garish walls, and clean floors.

Churches concerned about an environment that is appealing to both adults and children and that also conveys the gospel message have personalized their preschool and grade-school children's spaces in various ways that don't grow tiring, and for a lot less investment of money for "decorating."

- Several churches have designed display areas outside classrooms where children's "creations" can be displayed attractively and are changed often. Bulletin boards or strips, plastic frame holders, and other paper-gripping holders can be eye-catching and informative about what the children are learning in their classrooms or programs.
- Two churches the author visited have used squares of color on the hallway floors in different ways. One church had high-traffic carpet and inlaid geometric color squares at each room's entryway while another used tiles with color-accent squares spaced far enough apart that children cannot leap from block to block but still enjoy stepping on them day after day.
- A renovated preschool hallway in an urban church had groupings of three-to-five giant puzzle pieces with colorful pictures of children laminated on all but the lowest area of the wall, which was covered with a reflective material that mirrored the preschoolers walking by.
- A church in a suburb built a preschool and grade-school children's building that located the doors to the rooms so that four room doors clustered together, two on each side of the hallway, spaced to reduce crowding. At each door cluster is a large area of colored tiles in an accent color different from the rest of the hallway floor. The preschool room entrances used one accent color, and the grade-school children's room entrances used another one.
- Another creative church used a very colorful, wide stripe down the hallway walls. Rather than a straight line, a wide, angular line with peaks and valleys created interest.
- A church that wanted to display pictures of its children made large poster pictures and placed them in durable, plastic, frameless holders that were attached to the wall. The frames were constructed in such a way that the pictures could be changed periodically so that many children could have their pictures in the hallway over a period of time.

Murals are a popular hallway decoration. However appealing these might be at first, some issues need to be considered about murals in the hallway or in a classroom.

- Once murals are painted, they most likely will be there for a long time. Especially if someone in the church is the artist, nostalgia makes murals nearly permanent. The author has seen many deteriorating and dated murals in churches that do not have the heart to hurt anyone's feelings by painting over the mural. Professionally painted murals are usually very expensive, and churches want to get "their money's worth" by leaving them up long after they are no longer attractive. On the other hand, some amateur murals are not of good art quality even though they may have been "donated" by an artistic church member.

- Murals tend to be very large and some preschoolers are intimidated by gigantic (from their perspective) animals, faces, or even nature objects such as flowers. "Noah's Ark," a popular theme for preschool rooms, is about a flood that killed animals and people. In spite of God's rainbow promise, such a story can be very frightening to children who have experienced a flood or even a violent thunderstorm. A big fish that swallowed one of God's helpers (Jonah) can be intimidating as well.
- A preschool or grade-school room is the canvas on which the teaching session is "painted." The rooms are different from their rooms at home in that they should be prepared each session with the visual support for the lesson being taught that session rather than decorated with a theme that stays forever. A permanent mural of a Bible story in the room inhibits the learning of the content of that session, robbing the children of visual reinforcement.
- Some murals are idealized, cartoon-like portrayals of children (like "Precious Moments"). Children do not see themselves in that romanticized way, so the mural is for the benefit of the parents and teachers, not the children. And it is the children's room!

Churches would be better served by building larger rooms and providing attractive furnishings and teaching materials (even computers) rather than investing thousands of dollars in "decorations" that will need changing in a very few years to remain "fresh" and updated.

Are the rooms large enough to accommodate the number of children?

The smaller the child, the more space he or she needs because children are very active. Peering in the room, the parents wants to see enough space for their child to crawl, walk, or learn through active learning. Parents do not want to see preschoolers or grade-schoolers sitting around tables or vying for space.

A good guideline for the amount of room needed for preschoolers is 30 to 35 square feet per child for 80 percent of the enrollment. That gives the children room to move around without hurting themselves and others. It gives ample space to provide the teaching materials appropriate for each age group. With the younger preschoolers, beds as well as crawling space and rockers or gliders need to be accommodated. Toddlers need large muscle equipment such as a small indoor plastic slide or a modular climbing apparatus. Such equipment requires lots of room. Older preschoolers have many activity learning centers, such as home living furniture, large building blocks, an art table, and others. These centers require much space.

To accommodate active learning, grade-school children need 25 to 30 square feet per child for 80 percent of the enrollment. For children to have learning activity choices including drama, games, art, music, computers, and other methods that consider children's learning styles, they will need ample uncluttered room in which to learn creatively. Children should not be sitting around tables for the entire time of any one program.

If your space is too small, you can create more space by removing furniture or other large objects that are not essential. Rather than a table, grade-schoolers can write on a lapboard or clipboard. Even the floor can be used for seating if the space is exceptionally small. Many preschool and grade-school rooms are cluttered with unused furniture that is no longer used—upright pianos, dilapidated shelves or cabinets, baby swings or walkers, wrong-sized tables, etc.

Is the room a learning environment or a decorated environment?

Sometimes churches decorate preschool and grade-school children's rooms for the parents or adults rather than for the children. It is primarily a learning environment, not a child's bedroom or playroom. Consider these elements of a good learning environment for preschoolers and grade-schoolers at church:

- A cheerful, welcoming, child-attentive teacher is the most important element you can provide in a room!
- Rooms need outside light to enhance learning, not just for aesthetics. Minimal window treatments, if necessary, should let natural light come in to make God's world visually accessible as well as to boost learning. If blinds are used to control direct sunlight at certain times of the day, they need to be kept clean. If the room has few windows, make sure that the artificial lighting is adequate and of daylight quality.
- The walls should not be noticed when you enter a room. They should be painted a pleasant pastel or other somewhat pleasing color (rather than a bright, stimulating color) and not have permanent murals or pictures. Instead, the teaching materials, such as Bible pictures about the session's lesson, nature pictures, or the children's artwork, should be displayed at the eye level of the children in the room.
- Loudly colored carpet or boldly patterned tile or linoleum distracts preschoolers' or grade-schoolers' attention from the teaching materials. It also can overstimulate children of all ages, creating behavior problems in some children. Instead, upon entering the room, the children should be drawn to colorful and attractive learning materials such as books, blocks, pictures, games, and toys. Whether you choose a high quality carpet or tile for the rooms, the floors must be clean. Tile is easier to maintain, but it is noisier.
- The learning materials in the room need to be current and appropriate for the teaching purpose of the session. They should change often and stay current. Children (and adults) ignore familiar items after a few weeks. Changing them often stimulates children's interest. Bulletin

boards are not best for preschool rooms, as they require staples or pins, safety issues for preschoolers. Marker boards become ugly very quickly as children are very drawn to marking on them and churches do not clean them after every session. Chart paper is more effective as it can be used and thrown away at the end of the session.

- Furnishings and equipment need to be pleasantly colorful but not overpowering. For example, shelving, tables, and cabinets need to be neutral. Chairs may be a solid color such as navy, yellow, brown, or green. Remember that red, yellow, and orange are excitable colors and need to be used sparingly in permanent furnishings. The size of the furniture is important. Comfortable children, whose feet touch the floor rather than dangle, fidget less. Tables with light, washable tops are best. Five-foot rectangular tables are more flexible for grade-school children as they can be configured more easily than round or half-circle tables. Preschoolers need only one or two tables for art and perhaps puzzles or other manipulatives if you have adequate floor space to accommodate them.
- An uncluttered room arrangement is best for teaching even if your church has a weekday preschool program. Too many items in a room distract children. When the walls are covered with "colorful stuff" and items are dangling from the ceiling, it is overstimulating to children any time of the week.
- Cleanliness and safety are crucial. Floors, cabinets, and furniture need to be clean and in good repair. Childproof doors, covered outlets, cords out of a child's reach, shelving bolted to the wall, etc. will be noticed by parents. Unsafe items are liability issues for the church. Old furniture needs to be checked often for splinters or broken pieces and discarded if judged the least bit unsafe.
- Speakers or closed-circuit television should not be in the preschool rooms for the teachers to "monitor" the worship service. Remember that the teachers are to interact with the children and teach them. Listening to a worship service will distract them from meeting the needs of the preschoolers. Besides, as one elderly pastor said, "To the babies, I sound like a barking dog." In other words, the sounds from the worship center are not inviting to preschoolers and in some cases can be overstimulating.

Creating a Safe and Secure Environment for Children

Necessity of policies

"He [Jesus] took a little child and had him stand among them. Taking him in his arms, he said to them, 'Whoever welcomes one of these little children in my name welcomes me, and whoever welcomes me does not welcome me but the one who sent me'" (Mk. 9:36–37). "Welcoming" children today has new meanings. One aspect of "welcoming" minors (and their parents) in our world today is to make sure that we are protecting them from any kind of possible harm. Safety and security policies are a must, and churches finally are realizing it.

Advocates have been recommending safety and security policies for preschool and grade-school ministry for more than twenty years. So what has made churches so recently aware of risk management, causing them to pay urgent attention to safety and security issues and policies?

Media has made us aware of the magnitude of the vulnerability of children. News accounts of abuse incidents involving clergy, occurrences of teacher abuse in schools, and stories about abductions have heightened the awareness of the parents who now are demanding that churches demonstrate that their children will be safe. While the families already active in a church may believe that their children are safe with the teachers they have known for years, their beliefs may or may not be right, and unchurched families wisely do not blindly trust churches anymore.

Parents expect security measures in their child's daycare and/or school and require no less from any other institution and/or people caring for their children. If a church truly cares for children and is serious about protecting them, they need to have safety policies in place. Since the terrorist attacks in New York on September 11, 2001, awareness of security in general has changed the climate of businesses, airports, shopping malls, and other public places. Churches, which lock their doors during the week to protect the property and staff, must also be aware that the same precautions must be taken with the children and leadership when the church is meeting.

Insurance companies are increasingly refusing to renew or increase liability insurance for churches unless they have safety and security demonstrated with written (and enforced) policies, especially in regard to minors. They, too, recognize the importance of safeguarding the church and the children.

Security policies

Churches must formulate and enforce safety and security policies to safeguard children from predators, shield the church from litigation, protect leadership from false accusations, and provide ministry to families by giving them peace of mind whether they are visiting or in difficult family situations such as custody disputes.

All churches have the potential of being targeted by a child predator. Most people in churches are trusting by nature and assume that others attend church to worship God or to be with fellow believers. However, that trusting nature is exactly what pedophiles and others who wish to harm children rely on to allow them access to susceptible children. Most organizations servicing children (YMCA, Girl Scouts, Boy Scouts, etc.) now require background checks on personnel and risk management procedures when children are in their care. If churches do not do likewise, they will be an easy "mark" for abusive predators.

Churches must safeguard themselves from two types of perpetrators. The habitual molester will take time to build relationships of trust with children, often starting with small "tests" and increasing their "requests" for compliance incrementally. Criminal background checks will often identify these perpetrators. Criminal background checks on all volunteer and paid leadership involved with minors will identify convicted molesters, drug offenders, violent individuals, or careless drivers.

However, some people who do not have a conviction or who have yet to become a perpetrator will take advantage of a vulnerable situation. Background checks would not catch such a person, so churches must have other measures to protect the church, children, and leadership from a first offender (or previously uncaught offender). This is accomplished with several prudent measures:

- Requiring two nonrelated adults (18 years old or older) to be present with minors at all times (classrooms, hallways, bathrooms, vehicles, etc.) even if only one or two children are present
- Visual access to all areas of a room through a glass window in classroom doors
- Supervision in the hallways to protect the children and teachers from people who do not belong there
- Requiring active involvement or church membership of adults for six months before working with minors

Background checks of all volunteers will be an expensive endeavor, but it will be money well spent to protect the children and uphold the reputation of the church as a safe, caring place for children and their families. Similarly, never allowing an adult to be alone with children may seem overly protective to many church members. However, church leaders can never really know if their volunteers are truly safe; to think otherwise is to be in denial of the great threat present. And to risk a child's being abused is unthinkable.

Also, an accusation that cannot be disproved, whether it results in a conviction or not, ruins the reputation of a church for a long time. Good policies that are followed will protect the good name of the church in the community.

Every church must have a security system for preschoolers whenever they are out of the care of their parent(s). In other words, the parent signs the child into the classroom and is given an index card, laminated tag, or pager with the child's number on it (the one corresponding with the sign-in sheet). When the church event is over, the child will be given only to the parent with the corresponding security device. It takes intentional parent and teacher education about the procedure and adherence to the procedure for it to maintain its integrity. Failure to follow this strict procedure will result in security being compromised. Remember that such a security system will demonstrate to visitors that you are serious about the safety and security of their children, but regular attenders must follow the procedures as well for the system to be effective.

Visiting parents of young preschoolers or parents of infants in particular feel more secure with a pager system. If their child does not adjust to the new environment fairly quickly or becomes ill or needs feeding, parents can be easily summoned by a pager that vibrates or with a message board in the worship center that flashes the number of their child for that morning. Such safety measures can be distracting for some people, but the protection they provide for parents and for the church's reputation far outweigh the slight distractions they cause.

In addition to the security system, up-to-date child and family information cards that include family information as well as names of adults who are approved to pick up each child should be kept on file and be accessible only to authorized personnel. Some churches will choose to invest in the hardware for a high-tech "bar code" system of security, identification, and family attendance, but even a simple, inexpensive process is preferable to having nothing.

Accident prevention and safety

Accident prevention must receive priority attention in church buildings, especially in children's classrooms and hallways. Churches are notorious for overlooking glaring safety issues through benign neglect or inattentiveness. Open electrical outlets, cords hanging from CD players within easy reach of toddlers, exposed radiators and hot pipes, cribs and other furniture that do not meet current safety codes, exposed coat hooks at the eye-level of the children, looped blind cords, and too-small toys that could block a child's throat are a few of the safety issues churches often ignore until a child is injured. Broken toys or donated items from homes are often inappropriate for church use, yet they find their way into classrooms without screening.

Someone needs to be assigned the responsibility for evaluating the safety of each preschool and grade-school room each month. They will walk through the rooms when not in use and make notes of safety issues as well as ranking them in priority. Immediate concerns should be handled expeditiously and less serious matters can be dealt with in a timely manner. All leadership should report any immediate concerns to this designated person or the church office for handling. Making the rooms safe may cost the church money, but such expenses must be a priority if the church is to be faithful in caring for the welfare of its children.

Playground safety is another arena for a church's attention. Unsafe or broken equipment should be removed. The ground covering should be of adequate depth and material according to the recommendation of your state guidelines for licensed daycare centers. That guideline is for the protection of children who fall and should be the minimum that a church would be willing to provide for the safety of their children, whether it has a licensed childcare center or not.

Safety of preschoolers and grade-schoolers throughout the church is a priority as well. They will be in most of the church facilities with their parents at some time or another. A walk through the church with a child might uncover some of the safety issues that need attention.

Creating a clean environment for children

Churches wishing to reach families of young children must observe good hygiene. Several years ago ministers began noticing that parents were bringing their infants to the worship services rather than leaving them in the baby bedroom. When the author inquired in one of these churches why they kept the babies with them in the service, the parents indicated that their pediatrician had advised them not to put the infant in a church "nursery," because they were not clean. After checking with several churches, it was discovered that more than one pediatrician was giving that advice to parents. Sadly, they are correct about the poor hygiene practices in most churches.

A church that follows strict hygiene policies and informs parents of those procedures will attract families as well as provide a healthy environment for the babies and caregivers, too. Changing diapers with disposable gloves on waxed paper, and hand washing procedures will keep from spreading disease. Disinfecting toys, cribs, and other surfaces with a disinfecting solution will minimize the possibility of the church spreading germs from child to child. All toys in preschool rooms must be completely washable (no stuffed toys or cloth-body dolls). Leaders must be diligent to follow the disinfecting procedures after each session. With infants, disinfecting toys after each "mouthing" must be practiced, or germs are passed from child to child.

Even in the grade-school classrooms, use of gloves to handle runny noses and to disinfect surfaces will help to eliminate flu and cold epidemics among children and teachers, especially during the winter months. In addition, any blood loss must be handled with gloves. Disinfectant hand wipes or gel may be used by the grade-schoolers and teachers following each session if water is not available for hand washing with soap. First aid kits, telephones or pagers for emergencies, and fire escape procedures also help ensure that children and their teachers remain safe and secure and indicate to parents that the church values their children's safety.

Procedure for developing and implementing policies

A team, committee, or task force of church leaders guides the process of writing and implementing policies for preschoolers and grade-schoolers.

Team members need to include some key leaders from preschool, grade-school, and teen ministries and/or parents, as well as ministers for each of the age groups. It is also helpful to have a lawyer, human resources expert, law enforcement officer, medical personnel, or other professionals who might be able to provide expert information for the process.

This team will begin developing the policies by reviewing resources from organizations that deal with risk management. Several excellent organizations and resources are listed in appendix 7 of this book, and additional resources are available as well. The process of developing and implementing policies from beginning to end usually takes a year to eighteen months minimum, often longer.

After a thorough discussion of the issues and possible implications, the team will write customized policies for their church. The proposed policies should be taken to the decision-making body of your church for approval. Information or question/answer sessions with teachers, parents, and other interested persons will inform the congregation of the background, policies, and implementation plans. When the policies are approved according to your church approval procedures, written copies should be sent to every family.

A designated safety leader will be responsible for maintaining the confidential records associated with the policies: leadership applications, background check reports, driving records, and references. In addition, he or she also will be responsible for monitoring compliance with the policies and reminding those who are not following the policies of the importance of doing so.

"My room"

All of us like to have "our space," and children feel more secure when they are in familiar surroundings. David Elkind, a child psychologist and developmentalist, reminds us that children need space that is "theirs."[1] At church they need a place they can call "my room"—attractive, inviting, safe, and clean—full of people that show they care. It's just another way to say, "We love you," at an impressionable time in their lives.

Notes

[1]David Elkind, *Ties That Stress* (Cambridge, Mass.: Harvard University Press, 1994), 228–29.

CHAPTER 11

Is the Literature Meeting the Needs, Interests, and Development of the Preschoolers and Grade-schoolers?

The preschool teachers had been complaining for months about the literature they were expected to use for teaching Sunday school. When the new preschool director researched how the church had come to select the literature of that particular publisher, he found that the previous director had gone to the local Christian bookstore and chosen a literature favored by the salesperson. No teachers or ministers had provided input or evaluation. The church provided no training for its maximum use. Now, the new director wondered how he was supposed to choose a new literature from the dozen or so publishers at the bookstore and on the Internet.

The Literature Dilemma

Publishers have discovered the profitable consumer market for children's toys, books, clothing, and even church programs. In recent years dozens of Christian program materials for teaching preschoolers and grade-schoolers have been published and marketed to churches, ministers, leaders, and parents. Whether it is Bible study, discipleship, worship, or missions literature, learning experiences for children vary greatly. "Nutritional guidelines" do not appear on the products for good spiritual nourishment of preschoolers and grade-schoolers. That leaves untrained laypersons and busy ministers with little evaluative assistance.

For the purposes of this chapter, the *curriculum* for childhood ministry consists of all programs and experiences for preschoolers and grade-schoolers included in the total church experience. The curriculum of the church's childhood ministry comprises various *literatures* (i.e., books and other written resources) for the programs provided for the children plus church experiences.

A church that gives careful attention to literature selection will not let the teachers of classes make their own choices. Most literature will have a "scope and sequence" that cycles through the appropriate biblical stories and concepts in a certain number of years. In a curriculum approach, looking at the "scope and sequence" as well as how each of the program literatures reinforce and support what the church wants its preschoolers and grade-schoolers to know and experience is crucial. This makes literature selection critically important. For example, if the teachers simply choose what they want to teach, the children may learn some of the favorite Old Testament and Jesus stories, but will have very little teaching and learning about the early church or less dramatic biblical stories that still teach important truths.

People responsible for literature selection for the childhood ministry curriculum seldom think about some of the most important considerations. Often selections are made based on the attractive packaging, the clever theme, the publisher's appealing claims, a raving recommendation from another church, or even immediate availability. However, other criteria must be considered if a church wants to provide a balanced curriculum that will grow spiritually strong children. Be aware that seldom does a literature meet all of a church's criteria perfectly. However, when a church makes the choice of a literature that most nearly meets the priority criteria, they will be aware of the weaknesses, for which leadership will need training to compensate.

Criteria to Consider in Choosing Literature

Are the Bible stories doctrinally accurate and consistent with your church's teachings?

Not all "Christian" materials have the same doctrinal perspective or biblical account accuracy. The doctrine written into the literature is what most volunteer teachers will often teach. It is important that the doctrine of the literature reflects the teachings of your church so that the children will receive consistent messages throughout their church and family faith experiences. If the publisher has a denominational connection, the doctrine will reflect that perspective. Differences in perspective such as with baptism, communion, inspiration of Scripture, missions, the role of women in ministry, and other variances will be presented according to the denomination's doctrine. If the publisher is not affiliated with a denomination, such differences are often minimized to the extent that the teacher must include their church's teaching, an addition most often omitted because it is not written into the lesson plan.

Another consideration is whether the literature presents the biblical material accurately or takes liberties with the Scriptures. Some publishers will "embellish" the Bible stories but fail to qualify the additions to the biblical account. Instead of saying, "Jesus might have thought…," they will say, "Jesus thought…" Also consider the context of the Scripture to insure that it is accurately presented. The rule of thumb is that children should not be taught something that has to be changed later. Basic concepts are presented in their simplest form and built upon or expanded as the child can comprehend and apply more.

Are Bible content, learning activities, or other program information presented for children who are active in church, or will children who are not grounded in "church" be able to participate?

Think about the target audience for the literature selection. If it is being purchased for both preschoolers that do not know—as well as those who do know—about the Bible, Jesus, God, and other basic concepts, then look for assumptions. Often literature for older children will take for granted that the children have the basic concepts, and children who may be entering church for the first time will be "lost" in the language and depth of understanding. Other literature will be very basic and perhaps not challenging to children who have a rich church experience.

If the program is targeting preschoolers or children with limited church experience, then a literature with very basic concepts would be appropriate. Children who have attended church for years will need a challenging literature with lots of suitable learning experiences that encourage them to the next level of faith development. If the program anticipates a mixture of both churched and unchurched preschoolers and children, the mark of a healthy church constantly reaching new families, then the literature needs to have some guidance for the teachers in how to present the concepts to preschoolers or grade-schoolers with various levels of faith experience.

Are the understanding and skill levels of the pupils considered in the teaching suggestions and content?

As in other aspects of learning, preschoolers and grade-schoolers need to be exposed to concepts and learning activities that are age appropriate. Not all Bible stories contain appropriate content for young children. Long Bible verses or passages are not suitable in teaching young preschoolers or grade-schoolers either. If adults insist and are willing to spend the necessary time, some children can learn to recite large biblical passages even though they do not understand them. However, memorization today does not insure retention tomorrow.

Sometimes we assume that children understand what we are teaching, especially if we do not check what they are learning through their filters of understanding. Once I was teaching a group of second graders a lesson on prayer. At the end of the hour, we had a prayer time, applying what had been taught and hopefully learned. When I asked for prayer requests for others, one little boy asked for prayer for the "midgets." Not understanding his request, I asked a question to clarify. "Do you know any midgets?" I asked. "Yes, the ones upstairs," he replied. Then I understood that the boys' missions group had earlier in the morning delivered health kits to migrants, and this little boy had confused two words for which he had no understanding. I explained that the word was *migrant* and what the term meant.

A more effective teaching process involves teaching a child meaningful, applicable biblical truths and providing practical faith experiences that will reinforce the concepts. When evaluating literature, consider whether the content is too basic, too advanced, or beyond the experiential level of the children. The information being taught should be content that the preschooler or grade-school child needs to learn or experience to develop a better concept of and closer relationship with God right now. Meaningful learning is learning that provides a strong foundation on which future learning can be built.

Some publishers do not produce literature for preschoolers younger than two years of age. Brain research has shed light on the fact that much learning takes place in the first two years of life. In fact, the majority of the brain cells, which are only 25 percent connected at birth, are "wired" or linked to one another in the first five years of life. Much of that wiring takes place in the first two years as their environment stimulates children's senses. A rich church experience with teachers that talk and sing with babies while providing appropriate visual and auditory activities creates a nurturing, caring environment that also stimulates brain growth and faith development.

Rather than relying on someone else (a publisher) to determine what will be taught to the preschoolers and grade-schoolers in your church, use your own list of what you want your preschoolers and grade-schoolers to know and experience before they promote to the next age level. These concepts and experiences will provide focus for the teachers and parents and will ensure the church has guidelines for selecting literature that helps it accomplish its teaching/learning goals.

Perhaps the most common mistake made in childhood literature has to do with symbolic content. Until about the age of twelve, children are concrete, literal thinkers. However, many publishers use symbolic concepts such as "give your *heart* to Jesus" when they mean "give your life to Jesus," or "Jesus' little *lambs*" when they are not referring to a baby sheep. Watch for other abstract terms and concepts that do not make sense to literal-thinking children. If you explain the meaning of the abstract words, they can repeat what you say, but they do not understand how the symbol relates to the concept until they experience a shift in their thinking around the age of twelve.

Sometimes adults are convinced children understand the symbolism because they are attentively engaged in the activity and can answer the questions to which we have taught them the answers. If, however, you attempt to transfer the concept to another example, they quickly demonstrate their lack of understanding.

Some publishers are especially guilty of abstract, symbolic activities and stories. Whenever an object "is like" a concept that is not concrete, then abstract thinking is required. For example, if the Bible is like a bandage because it must be opened to be useful, or colors represent sin and forgiveness, or music lyrics say "let your light shine" or "open your heart's door," then abstract concepts are being presented. To be concrete and understood by children, objects must be themselves.

Is literature pupil-centered (child-friendly) rather than teacher-centered?

Many times, literature is selected because it is very easy for the teacher to prepare. Often what is easily prepared is not appealing or helpful to the child. A literature that employs many color sheets, worksheets, stickers, and patterned art or craft activities is a teacher-centered literature. Teacher-centered literature usually involves a lot of "teacher talking" and "student listening" rather than substantive dialogue between teacher and child or conversation among the children. In addition, the teacher is the expert, and the children are the learners, in a teacher-centered classroom.

Child-centered literature lets children participate in the teaching process. Teachers that ask thought-provoking questions that generate thinking and dialogue rather than asking questions that have expected answers will find that children can be teachers, too. The author has discovered profound insights through the questions and thoughts of children in a child-centered teaching/learning experience. One older child asked at the end of the story of the first murder, when Cain killed his brother Abel, "If it was the first time, how did they know they could do it?" That one, thoughtful question opened a fertile dialogue of the source of Cain's anger, God's caution to Cain about his anger, and how sometimes when we are angry we lash out to others without intending harm, but harm them nevertheless. Self-control is a difficult life skill, especially for children; but this dialogue generated thoughts that if they did not "master their anger," they, too, were capable of harming someone, even someone they loved.

Child-centered literature also gives preschoolers and grade-schoolers choices of how they will learn. If everyone does the same thing at the same time and everything that is made looks like all of the others, it is a teacher-centered activity. The child-centered teacher intentionally guides the learning that takes place through the activities, but the child chooses from the methods provided to learn the content. Through active learning, exploring, creating, and interacting, preschoolers as well as grade-schoolers experience the content in a way that has the most meaning and retention for them.

Are sound educational approaches used, or are the teaching methods primarily "busy work"?

Learning should be fun, but not all fun is learning. Sound educational methods have a learning component that is more than simply being told a story and answering questions about the facts of the story. That is the beginning of learning, but it is the lowest level. Coloring a picture or sticking a sticker on a page fills time and requires minimal preparation, but these "activities" contribute little to a child's faith understanding or development, even if they like to color and lick stickers.

Children need to be asked thoughtful questions beginning with phrases such as the following:

I wonder what _____ might have felt about…?

What if…?

What would have happened if…?

If you had been there, what would you have…?

Teachers need to be careful that activity actually involves learning, and is not simply busy work. Crafts that have a pattern for everyone to follow or worksheets to fill in the blanks keep the children active but are boring for most children. *The goal of a good teaching session is that the preschooler or grade-schooler will leave with information and experiences that will change his or her life, not that they will have something in their hands to give their parents for the refrigerator.*

Are the learning methods and activities varied and interesting to preschoolers and grade-schoolers?

Some people learn better visually. They want to "see" pictures, words, and faces. Others prefer to "hear" words, music, and sound effects. Other people need to involve their body in learning as they form clay models, play an active game, or act out a story. A child-centered literature gives options for a variety of learning styles so the teachers can choose the options that appeal to the children in their class rather than the options that appeal to the teachers.

On average, people of any age usually retain only 10 percent of what they hear, but they retain 90 percent of what they do if the "doing" is meaningful. Involvement of multiple senses in a learning experience insures better retention as well. Since repetition of a concept through a variety of sensory experiences has been proven as a very strong teaching practice, literature that appropriately includes multiple senses in each session should be considered. As with other activities, sensory experiences can be "fillers" without much life impact.

Preschool literature needs to suggest active learning choices, preferably in activity centers such as art, home living or dramatic play, puzzles and manipulatives, or blocks, based on one major concept for that session. Since the attention span of young children is about one minute for every year of age, preschool classrooms need to have more activity time than group time. Preschoolers younger than three should not be expected to "sit and listen" in a group setting. For children younger than three years of age, the teaching of the story and Bible thoughts and verses occurs as the teacher interacts with preschoolers in activities designed to reinforce the concept for the day.

Likewise, grade-school children should not be expected to "sit and listen" for the entire lesson either. Learning activities involving art, music, drama, creative writing, games, and other teaching methods allow a child to be creative while applying the Bible truth for the session. The best learning occurs when a child actually understands how the Bible truth applies to his or her life and implements that truth.

Do the learning activities impact the child's knowledge, feelings, and behavior?

Many of the publishers of literature for preschoolers and grade-school children emphasize teaching information. While knowledge is basic and very important, equally significant is exploring their feelings related to spiritual matters as well as affecting their behavior to be Christ followers. In evaluating how effectively this is done, look for conversations, learning activities, and worship experiences that consider the child's knowledge, feelings, and behavior in their content.

Does the literature include teaching suggestions for children who have learning disabilities or physical challenges, as well as for children who are gifted?

Not all children are "average." Preschoolers and grade-schoolers with special needs or gifts often are mainstreamed with other children in church ministries or programs. To assist teachers in adapting the learning environment or content for a physically or mentally challenged child or a very gifted child, literature should have suggestions for adjusting the learning experiences. The author once taught a fourth grade child who was blind. His mother read his lesson to him before each Sunday and the teachers chose or adapted learning activities that encouraged him to be an active learner along with the other children. Our literature gave enough suggestions that we were able to make our own adjustments once we had some guidance in the early months.

Some churches are providing special classes and literature for children with special needs and are bringing the other children into their classrooms for some of the teaching time. This reverse mainstreaming takes into account the special needs of all children while giving the specialized attention needed as well. Also, if you teach multiple age groups that are younger or older than the age for which the literature is targeted, does the literature give some help for adjusting the teaching methodology for older or younger children? Even if all of the children are the same age, not all of them will be functioning on the same academic level, and suggestions for adjusting the difficulty of the activities is helpful to the inexperienced teacher.

Is the literature attractive to preschoolers or grade-school children?

If the teaching resources are not appealing to preschoolers and grade-schoolers, or if they are too juvenile for the age group, they will not have the optimum learning impact. Colorful, realistic artwork best conveys the reality of the message we are teaching. Since young children have difficulty distinguishing between reality and fantasy, it is in their best interest to provide illustrations that are not caricatures of biblical stories or present-day children. When Bible characters look like the cartoons on television, it is difficult for a child to perceive that these were once real people just like them. Realistic art reinforces the truth of the gospel message visually.

However, the art needs to be appealing and attractive to preschoolers or grade-schoolers. If it looks too juvenile, older children will feel patronized. If it is too graphic or scary for preschoolers, they will not be "invited" into the story. Good art for children has simple lines, appealing color, and emphasizes the important part of the Bible story. Zacchaeus might have been small in stature, but that isn't the point of the story any more than David cutting off Goliath's head is the part of the story we want the grade-schoolers to remember. What is pictured is often what they will remember.

Are worship opportunities included in the teaching plan?

Some publishers seem to develop lessons full of frenzied activities and games in the pursuit of fun and entertainment. Little if any time is suggested for contemplation or reflection. Some lesson plans do not recommend prayer, singing, or even Scripture reading. Today's preschoolers and grade-schoolers are bombarded with constant media and scheduled activities and have very little encouragement to "be still and know that I am God."

A balanced faith, whether for adults or children, will have worship times with active praise. Even preschoolers and grade-schoolers need opportunities to consider the wonder of God and their relationship to God in quieter moments.

How is evangelism presented?

Some publishers never give guidance in their literature about how to talk with a child about the conversion experience. Others use excessive coercion, manipulation, and repetition in their lessons for preschoolers and grade-schoolers. Still others use abstract and symbolic language and stories that children do not understand, but which appear very entertaining.

For preschool literature, search for a publisher that guides the teachers in laying the foundations necessary for the young child to understand the basic gospel message. Concepts such as God, Jesus, Bible, prayer, church, worship, and other basic ideas should be explained in simple yet accurate language. A good literature will start preschool lessons with the basics of each biblical or theological concept and build on it, depending on the understanding, development, and experience of the child.

Literature for grade-school children should continue to enlarge the preschool concepts as well as help them to know the basic story of redemption and how they might choose to respond to the Holy Spirit when the time comes. In addition, the literature should help the teacher who needs to know how to counsel a child using terms that the child will comprehend. An added benefit to look for is how to talk with parents about *their* faith journey. Remember that the church is to support the home faith teaching, so any guidance that can be given parents about their spiritual growth will ultimately benefit the child. Avoid literature that compromises the truthful impact of Scripture by using puppets, clothed animals, talking animals, cartoons, or even legends to teach the biblical lessons. A reality-based approach delivered by a teacher of faith reinforces the authentic message being taught.

What support resources are available to make it easier for teacher preparation?

Much excellent literature requires a lot of the teacher's time for preparation. Volunteers who are busy in all aspects of their lives will not spend a lot of time in preparing teaching resources even if the lesson is excellent. To teach in an active, hands-on way, teachers need *prepared* materials that will encourage them to involve the children in meaningful, energetic learning on a high level.

Look for lessons that provide realistic teaching pictures and meaningful teaching items, not just busy work or crafts. Evaluate whether the support items simply "fill time" or whether they assist in meaningful learning. For example, is the resource item simply a coloring page, a picture on which a child sticks a sticker, or a "craft" that involves very little learning, or is it a higher level of learning such as an activity, game, or drama to teach a Bible verse or make an application of the Bible truth? While coloring or sticker pages or "cutsie" crafts may be easy to prepare, they add little to the children's biblical knowledge or experience.

Additional items such as maps of Bible lands, music CDs, preschool activity center accessories, small books, and CD-ROMs encourage varied learning experiences that appeal to the different learning styles of children. These teaching resources may take some minimal preparation, but the learning the children will experience will encourage the teachers.

Literature varies in the amount of encouragement for teachers to grow in their faith journey and teaching ability as well. Teachers that experience personal improvement through additional Bible background material and practical teaching tips become stronger and more effective teachers.

CHAPTER 12

Does Your Church Have a Council, Committee, or Team to Support the Preschool and Grade-school Ministry?

The author remembers the first coordinating group on which she served. The church was a new church start sponsored by four churches. The fledgling preschool and grade-school ministry needed much support because of the sizeable number of families with young children who came to the church. When the "council" was formed, we suddenly had a core of people who were planners and advocates for the preschoolers, grade-schoolers, and families, as well as the church's ministry to them. Indeed, "six heads" were better than one!

The coordinating council, committee, or team is an official, perhaps elected group. They have as their priority the faith development of the preschoolers and grade-school children. They also oversee childhood ministries, leaders, facilities, policies, and families. In other words, since children do not have a voice in most churches, this group looks out for their interests and needs to make sure the children are provided the best ministry the church can possibly offer.

Composition of Coordinating Group

Many churches begin with a combined preschool and grade-school coordinating group. However, preschool concerns are very different from grade-school concerns. As a church's preschool and grade-school ministries grow, often the two age groups each need their own coordinating body to better use their time for issues that concern the whole group. Preschool teams must deal with more security policies and hygiene concerns as well as worship care and other childcare concerns, while grade-schoolers require more "extra" planned events outside of the regularly programmed ministries.

The next decision involves the type of coordinating group the church will form. A *council* usually includes one primary leader from each of the major ministries or programs for the preschoolers and grade-schoolers and sometimes a few other people, often parents. A *committee* or *team* may be composed of people who are willing to give the time and energy to these age group ministries. The most effective coordinating groups include both the primary leaders of the major ministries (for the purpose of coordinating the ministries) and parents or other interested adults. The ministry leaders are investing major time and energy in their program responsibilities, so additional people who can pick up some of the extra responsibilities as well as offer other points of view or perspectives are valuable.

Here are some possible members:

- A key Sunday school or Bible study leader
- Discipleship organization leaders (examples: Bible Drill, TeamKid, AWANA, etc.)
- Key mission group leaders for boys, girls, or co-ed groupings
- Choir or music leader
- Weekday preschool and/or after-school program coordinator or director
- Three or four parents (mothers and fathers from different families);
- Childcare coordinator
- Worship leader (preschool worship care and/or children's worship leader)
- Staff liaison
- A representative from any other church program or ministry for children

Some churches include older children on a grade-school coordinating group. One or two fifth or sixth graders could attend some of the meetings and give input when it is appropriate. They also could help to plan some of the events sponsored by the group. It is important for coordinating group members to have an interest in and commitment to the ministry with preschoolers, grade-schoolers, and their families. These people must not have their own agenda, but rather must be able to work well with others to accomplish a common task.

General Responsibilities

1.To determine and recommend to the church the overall objectives and emphases for the preschool and/or grade-school ministry

To make plans for the upcoming church year, the coordinating group will meet for an extended period of time (perhaps an all-day or overnight retreat) to evaluate the current ministry to children and their families and to determine the objectives and ministry focus for the new church year. This planning event needs to occur by April or May of each year if the programming changes in the fall. This coordinating group does more than schedule activities for the year. Consideration should be given to successful ministries that you want to maintain and strengthen, ministries that are weak and need strengthening or eliminating, and ministries that are not being provided but are needed. Base the planning on leadership resources, financial resources, space resources, as well as the input and response of children and families to current ministry and expressed needs.

If the coordinating group is newly formed and has no agreed-on vision for the childhood ministry, the first task is developing the vision (see chapter 1). If there is a vision for the church and the childhood ministry, the committee needs to revisit the vision and ask questions:

- Why are we doing each of the present ministries? Are they ministries that help us attain our stated vision, or are they just activities?
- What does this church need to provide for the children and parents in our church and our community that no one else is offering? Why?
- Is God calling us to do something that seems challenging? What is our first step in responding to that challenge?
- How much can we do effectively?
- When the preschoolers are promoted into the grade-school age group, what do we want them to know and have experienced?
- When the grade-schoolers become teens, what do we want them to know and have experienced?
- What will be our focus for this year? (*Examples:* Intergenerational [family] activities, worship education and guidance, leadership training, reaching the community through new approaches, mission events, parent seminars, etc.)

2. To recommend policies to the church body that will assure quality teaching, guidance, and safety for children every time they attend church

If the church does not have safety and security policies, then this group would be the one to initiate and encourage that process; however, the members may not comprise the entire group that formulates the policies. It is a labor-intensive process that needs a support base broader than this coordinating group. If a church does have safety and security policies implemented, this group has such involvement in every aspect of the ministry that they could be charged with the responsibility of identifying weaknesses, oversights, or new issues that may need to be addressed. They might recommend changes to existing policies even though the original policy formulating committee may need to formally recommend amendments to the policies and procedures.

3. To coordinate the activities of departments, classes, groups, and ministries to children and their parents. All preschool and grade-school activities will be cleared through this committee and coordinated with the church calendar

To provide a reasonable, balanced, and orderly scheduling of activities as well as to avoid overscheduling children and families, all ministries must have the activities outside of their regularly scheduled time presented, approved, and calendared by the coordinating group. That means that advanced planning and regular meetings are required.

4. To coordinate the assignment and use of space and equipment

Since many organizations and groups normally use the same teaching rooms, all of the organizations' leadership need to agree on use of wall space, placement of furniture, and use of supplies. At the beginning of each church year, the leadership of all organizations using a room should meet and agree on the above-mentioned usage. The coordinating group should facilitate this process and encourage dialogue and cooperation among all of the program leaders.

5. To recommend the purchase of furnishings, supplies, repairs, and renovations

When new items are needed, a written request needs to be made to the coordinating group. The committee will approve the request and make a formal request to the church entity responsible for purchasing. Sometimes the coordinating group will need to work with all of the organizations to determine what is needed or not needed. For example, if one teacher wants another table added to a room, but the space is inadequate to accommodate another table with current attendance in another organization using the room, then the committee will work with the request and make a recommendation that is best for all organizations.

6. To communicate regularly with the church coordinating body about ministries that affect preschool and grade-school work

The chairperson of this coordinating group will serve on the church coordinating body and communicate needs, plans, and activities for approval and coordination with other activities/ministries of the church. If the church does not have a church coordinating body, the chairperson will work with the childhood minister/director or another staff member who is the liaison with the staff to communicate the needs and plans of the childhood coordinating body.

7. To supervise the work of the event teams if your church uses event teams to conduct activities not a part of your ongoing programs

Some churches have adapted for childhood ministry an event process based on Richard Ross's "Lead Team" concept for youth.[1]

- After the coordinating group plans the overall ministry for the upcoming year, including the goals and emphases of the year and the ministries and activities that will meet those goals, they are ready to form the event teams. The identified activities that do not fall under the guidance of one of the ongoing ministry programs would then be assigned to one of the event teams. Those events could include such things as teacher appreciation activities, seasonal parties and fellowships, vacation Bible school, outreach activities and ministries, family events, day camp or residential camp experiences, etc. The coordinating group determines the events for the year and sets a budget. The event teams will implement the plans.

- The next step involves parents, teachers, and other interested adults being invited to a meeting in which these events are presented. (Some churches have found they can reach the most people through a luncheon after the Sunday morning worship service or a snack supper before another planned church activity.) Place large sheets of paper around the wall with each activity or ministry written on the top along with the date–if the coordinating group has chosen a date. (Some churches let the event team choose the exact date within an assigned month and go through the coordinating group chair or childhood minister to get it placed on the church calendar.) Down the left side of the paper, write the numbers for the number of people needed for each event team. After introducing the year's plans and briefly explaining each activity or ministry, parents and other interested volunteers sign up for at least one and no more than two events. Leave the unfilled sign-up sheets in a prominent place so that people who may not have been able to attend the initial meeting will be able to sign up in the next two weeks. You might want to put a brief written description and expectations of each activity or ministry next to each sign-up sheet.

- A mixture of parents, teachers, other interested adults, and possibly some older children comprise the event teams. Fifth and sixth graders are especially interested in assisting with events, and this gives them a special opportunity that can help transition them to youth. The size of the event team depends on the magnitude of the assignment. Generally, five or six people make a good event team planning group. They may enlist others to assist with special aspects of the event or activity.

- After the sign-up time, event teams will meet briefly and elect a leader. Persons on more than one team may need to choose to meet here for the event that is scheduled first.

- Set up monthly meetings for all of the event teams. Each team should meet in the same room each time. This scheduled time helps people to be accountable and faithful. This also allows the childhood minister and/or coordinating group members to go from group to group, checking on the plans and offering information when needed. As each event team completes their project, they will no longer meet. Those event teams whose event may be nearer the end of the year may not meet as often early in the year, but will need to be encouraged not to wait until the last minute either. Each event team is given a budgeted amount within which they must make their plans. If they

need additional funds, they will need approval from the coordinating body before spending it. Some events may not require the full budget allotted, so the amounts may be transferred as the year progresses.
- The role of the coordinating group members is to guide the work of the event teams. They may be on one or more of the event teams if necessary, or they may be the emergency "fill-ins" if team members drop out or do not follow-through with their commitment. The coordinating group members are not to chair the event teams nor do the work while the event team "helps."

8. To develop "ministry partners" that can enhance the childhood ministry and be supporters of the ministry

Childhood ministry can become isolated and in some cases "invisible." The coordinating group needs to build alliances with other groups in the congregation that can support and even strengthen the preschool and grade-school ministry:

Senior adult ministry
- Alliances can be established with the senior adult ministry or even Sunday school classes to provide interaction between the senior adults and the preschoolers and grade-schoolers. Events can be scheduled that involve the two groups, or a network can be established between children and senior adults. Some planning teams have organized "Secret Angels" at Christmas, tutoring programs staffed with senior adults, special events like picnics and musicals involving children and seniors, parent mentors, and prayer partners for the school year.
- Faith family grandpas and grandmas can be powerful advocates for the childhood ministry when they know what is going on and are in relationship with the children and families. Likewise, parents might be advocates for the senior adult ministry when they interact with the seniors rather than being isolated from them.

Student or teen ministry
- Teens do not need to be the primary caregivers for the children at church. However, programming that involves the youth in some of the preschool and grade-school activities can be beneficial for the teens and the children. In one church the youth planned and conducted the fall festival for the children, including the food and games. In other churches they might be tutors, trained and certified (by the church) babysitters in the homes, or big brothers/big sisters to the children being promoted into the teen ministry.

Outreach ministry
- Any group that is representing the church to the community needs to be fully informed about the childhood ministries. Make sure that

they have brochures about the regular church programming as well as any special upcoming events. An outreach strategy that highlights preschool and grade-school ministry will catch the attention of young families.

This coordinating group needs to believe that what they are doing is vitally important to the success of the ministry and the life of the preschoolers and grade-schoolers. It could be seen as "extra work" if it is just an "activities planning group." As they support and encourage each other in their various programs, think of creative ways to enhance the faith formation of children and families, and involve even more people in the ministry's special events, they will see the ministry grow and flourish and see themselves as vital servants in God's work.

Notes

[1]Ross's approach is discussed in Dwayne Ulmer, *Basic Student Ministry in Kingdom-Focused Churches* (Nashville: Church Resources, 2003).

CHAPTER 13

Whatever You Are Called, Are You Called?

What's in a Name?

Churches have a variety of titles for both the volunteer and paid preschool and/or grade-school ministers. Here are some of the most common ones:

Laypersons and sometimes-paid staff

Children's Director
Preschool Director
Director of Children's Ministries
Director of Preschool Ministries
Director of Childhood Education
Preschool Ministry Coordinator

Paid staff positions

Associate Pastor of Children
Assistant Minister of Children
Preschool and Children's Minister
Children's Pastor
Children's Minister or Preschool Minister
Minister with Children
Minister to Children
Minister of Children or Minister of Preschool

Associate Minister for Preschool and Children
Minister of Childhood Education
Minister with Children and Families
Children's Educational Director
Minister to Families
Associate Minister to Students
Minister to Youth
Family Life Minister
Associate Pastor for Family

God's Call

"Calling" is often equated to a testimony when others ask about it, but it is multifaceted and often multilayered. A calling, whether as a layperson or paid staff, begins with God and a personal relationship with God. A minister's first calling occurs when he or she comes into relationship with God through a decision to follow Christ instead of his or her own desires.

The call to ministry, however, seems to occur in a variety of ways and may be a calling to church ministry or marketplace ministry. It may have been a single, focused moment; or, it may have been a series of events, or even a gradual surrender. Some calls may be associated with a person's gifts, the realization and path seeming to flow naturally from those gifts. Others find that their call came in the midst of a need that produced an opportunity for them to respond and use the gifts God had given them. Perhaps they were a parent responding to a needed teaching position. They may have started out of "duty" as a parent, but found a joy in service that lasted long beyond their call to "duty." For others, the call is somewhat mystical, as they perceive the very voice of God, making it unmistakable that this is where God wants them to invest their time and abilities.

Calling to preschool or grade-school children's ministry involves a passion—a heart passion. You must feel and know that ministry with children is what you have to do because that is where God wants you to be. It can be a very difficult ministry at times even if you are called to it. With your calling and passion comes much strength to be the best minister you can be. First Samuel 10:9 reports that Saul had a "changed heart" after his anointing by Samuel as the first king of Israel. It was not a conversion experience but a change in character and strength to fulfill God's calling in his life. That is what a calling from God does for a minister today as well. It is a willingness to be what God wants you to be so you can rely on God to give you the strength and wisdom to do the ministry.

A calling to childhood ministry is a fairly new concept in recognized professional ministry. People, especially women, have always functioned as preschool or grade-school directors, but they were not "on" the church staff, paid as a minister, or, in some cases, officially elected to the position.

They did it because they felt that God wanted to use them in his kingdom, they were gifted to do it well, and they were passionate about the ministry. These people have had a profound impact on children and churches for decades, but were never acknowledged as ministers.

Whether a church chooses to recognize the preschool and grade-school leader as a minister is not the issue. A leader called by God is a minister and should conduct the ministry with that outlook. God calls and uses whom he chooses for his work, not always those whom others think he chooses. However, verification of that calling will come from the body as they affirm and acknowledge the benefit of the ministry to the faith family.

The author's first full-time ministry position was as the Director of Childhood Education in a large urban church. It also was the first paid childhood education staff position in the history of the church. However, for many decades a woman had volunteered as the coordinator of the education programs for the preschoolers and grade-school children. The church had no idea how many hours she had contributed to the outstanding teaching ministry of the church. Still, with the church finally creating a new "minister" position dedicated to these younger age groups, plus adding training, resources, and events, the church enhanced the faithful foundation that this dedicated volunteer, who no doubt was called by God, had supplied.

Being a childhood minister is not easy. "Ministry storms" will come– from parents, church leadership, staff, maybe family. Sometimes it is criticism, disappointment in leadership, crisis events in the church or at home, or maybe just not feeling appreciated. Other times will bring sunshine experiences when you bask in the glow of successful ministry or relationships. It takes both rain and sunshine to make a rainbow. A rainbow cannot occur without the raindrops that take the sunlight and diffuse it into a spectrum of color. Our ministry will always have storms, but we have the choice of being like the raindrops that diffuse the stormy clouds into colors of ministry. That is not always easy. We think we would like constant sunshine experiences in a successful ministry, but the storm experiences will come. We can choose to view these storms as opportunities for ministry too.

The way the minister expresses his or her call and passion will shape that person's ministry. The church often "expects" a certain kind of ministry emphasis. One of the challenges is for the minister and the congregation to have the same passion and expectations of expressed ministry.

Some ministers have gifts and passions for ministry expressed as:

Healer

Most churches have people carrying deep hurts from their pasts. Some persons have dealt with the pain, but others carry it with them into every relationship. The healer minister will give priority to the pastoral care needs of children and parents such as life crises, life changes, or even small emotional disturbances. Some churches are carrying corporate pain from past group divisions that have not been healed. Rather, the church pushed the pain aside only to see it resurface in another inevitable conflict. Healing ministers are not intimidated by conflict but are able to deal with the hurt and help persons and congregations move to health and wholeness so that God's kingdom can be the focus once again.

Builder

The builder minister is usually effective in organization as well as relationships. He or she first builds a network of personal relationships, then creates a supportive system of relationships among parents, teachers, and children. A ministry that has satisfying and rich relationships attracts people, and often the organization begins to grow. A builder enjoys building an organization because it can accommodate more relationships, and the "building" continues to produce more relationships.

Mentor

The mentor minister is often a good nurturer whom others repeatedly choose to be their mentor. For example, a teacher in a church program might choose the minister as a mentor if he or she perceives that the minister could guide him or her to be a more effective teacher. A struggling parent may revere a minister's parenting skills and choose the minister as a mentor. Some ministers are just exceptionally good mentors.

Manager

Some churches value and seek a minister/leader who is a very effective administrator—successful in enlisting leadership and organizing programs and events so that they run very smoothly. These ministers want everything done "decently and in order" with a minimum of glitches. This type of minister actually enjoys the administrative details involved in preschool and grade-school children's ministry.

Combination

Most ministers are by necessity a blend of all of these types, but most ministers gravitate toward one of the above ministry emphases. Sometimes the church's expectations push in one direction, and the minister feels more passion or giftedness in another. The goal is to find a ministry position in which the expectations of the church and your ministry expression are a match.

Ultimately, it is not what you know or do but who you are that will determine your success in ministry. Being your best is a priority and a point of integrity. Your ministry is like no one else's. God has uniquely gifted you, and your life experiences and learnings will impact your distinctive ministry. Consider whether you are *being* the best "you" that you can be, or are you merely *doing* your best? A balance of being and doing is vital in ministry.

Acceptance of God's Call

Ministry's deep taproot is relationships. Ministers who do not have high-quality relationships with God, children, parents, age group teachers/ leaders, church staff, and other church leaders will find that they burn out or change jobs often.

Relationship with God

Ministers give so much time and energy to the demands and expectations of others that they must be refueled or they will "run dry." Ministers will get so involved in *doing* that they can forget to *be*. Most ministers experience the increasing pace of life that seems to escalate with each passing year. How many times do you hear or say, "I don't have time to…"? The nature of ministry is that it is never complete or even "caught up." How much time are you giving God, who does not demand it as others do, but who gives it and desires your undivided attention not only for God's sake, but for your sake as well?

Ministers must want to make time with God so much that they will make it a priority in their extremely busy lives. Bible study, meditation, prayer, and other spiritual disciplines enrich the "God connection" and keep the ministries focused on the important priorities. When that relationship with the Eternal is right, then they are ready to be in relationship with those to whom they are called to minister.

Relationships with children

Churches need ministers in the "mission field," relating to people, rather than just running programs, activities, and meetings. Parents in our unchurched culture are looking for people who exhibit genuine care for their children. The programs and activities are nice, but what they really seek are relationships that are genuine and meaningful.

Ministers with these age groups must be able to relate to preschool and grade-school children. They are drawn to this ministry because of their passion to share their faith with preschoolers and/or grade-schoolers. That heart for children makes these ministers very good advocates for their ministry, promoting what is good and right for preschoolers and grade-schoolers even when others are determined to put other interests ahead of what is best for the children.

Children must know, even sense, that we love them. The author was having breakfast with an interim pastor while planning an Easter service. A little boy walked past the table and I must have smiled at him. He stopped his father and proceeded to show me the picture he had drawn and tell me all about it when I asked. As the embarrassed father dragged the little boy away even while he continued the conversation, the pastor said, "Even strange children sense that you love them." I could not have received a higher commendation, but indeed, I do.

Relationships with parents

Parents in our unchurched culture are looking for ministers who not only demonstrate genuine care for their children but also desire someone who can offer them assistance in child rearing and nurturing so they can become better parents. An effective preschool and/or grade-school children's minister is indeed a family minister. The minister needs to be viewed as the parents' strongest ally and supporter. Regular communication and interaction with parents is a priority in building relationships with them. Visiting in their homes and participating in the adult ministries of the church when possible will only strengthen those relationships. The children's minister must set up a scheduling priority to be present in the vicinity of the preschool and grade-school activities when the parents are accompanying their children. Ministers must greet parents as well as children.

Relationships with teachers and leaders

Much of your ministry is with adults rather than children. In addition to assisting parents, preschool and grade-school children's ministers must enlist, train, encourage, and develop relationships with teachers and leaders. Nurturing relationships with teachers and leaders involves demonstrating that you really care about *them,* and not only what they do. It includes giving them permission to take a break from their responsibilities without making them feel guilty when they need to shift their priorities due to circumstances in life. Remember that the ministry is not "yours." You are a minister to teachers and leaders as well as the preschoolers and grade-school children.

Relationships with staff

Whether your position is considered a staff position or not, whether you are paid for your ministry or not, be a good team player with the church staff. Nurture those staff relationships so that the preschool and grade-school ministry piece fits into the total ministry plan for your church. Cooperation and negotiation is much more effective than fighting for what you need.

A minister in her first staff position called the author several years ago, complaining that the pastor would not let her do conversion counseling with the children who were indicating that they wanted to follow Jesus. She felt that because of her position, she had the right to do the counseling. After informing her that she had no rights in that congregation if the senior pastor didn't assign the responsibility to her, we devised a scenario of what she would do with a child, the parents, and the senior pastor if she were the initial counselor with the child and family. The pastor readily agreed to her plan after he was assured of her process and content, and their working relationship was further strengthened.

Respect for a person's ministry is earned—not just given to a position, title, or degree—in most church staffs as well as congregations. It comes through building relationships as you work side by side, interacting with other ministers and showing mutual respect.

Relationships with other childhood ministers and/or Christian educators

Many new preschool and grade-school children's ministers enter a ministry position from the laity, knowing they lack preparation for the ministry. Many of these have found that finding a mentor minister can give good guidance and support. Mentors often have resources that have been helpful in their ministry. Increasingly, ministers who have coaching skills can be helpful in coaching a new minister. Check around your city, town, or region for childhood minister groups that meet regularly to exchange information, do continuing education, or simply offer support and encouragement to each other. Meeting with ministers responsible for general Christian education would be helpful as well in exploring how other churches "do ministry" in their settings.

What you "do" in ministry will be against the backdrop of your relationships. People will be more forgiving of your inadequacies or mistakes in ministry actions if you have a good relationship with them. Calculate the time you spend developing relationships against the time spent doing the "ministry stuff" you have to do. Make sure that the weight is in favor of relationships.

Life-sharing Ministry

You have life experiences that will shape and form your ministry even as you learn from them. Much of the "heart" of your ministry will come from those experiences. I do not believe that God causes bad things to happen to make us better ministers, but I do think that our spiritual responses to our life experiences, just because we are human, can and will shape the most powerful encounters in our ministry.

When the author was 30 years old, I was diagnosed with cancer. It was operable, but it recurred seven times before it stopped redeveloping. As a result of what I learned from that personal and difficult experience, I have become a "wounded healer" to other people who are facing or battling cancer. As a result of having cancer, I faced my mortality at an early age. I became a consumer of books and resources on ministry during death experiences (involving both adults and children). So when the 7-year-old daughter of my church's pastor and minister of education and youth was killed in a wreck caused by a drunk driver, I was able to respond to the church children, the adults, and even the family of the dead child with a preparedness that I would not have had without the reading and reflection I had done to deal with my own mortality.

Each minister will probably have his or her own significant personal life experiences, such as the death of a parent at a young age, birth of a child, divorce of parents, or abusive treatment. You have a unique perspective and hopefully spiritual insight and wisdom that can help you in your ministry with children or even with parents experiencing the same difficult circumstances. To be helpful, you must have a healthy perspective of your personal crisis (or crises). If you continue to struggle with the experience(s), seek some professional help, an objective perspective to help you work through a tough life experience. Many good Christian counselors can help you sort through the minefields that sometimes accompany difficult life situations. A more experienced minister may be able to provide words of wisdom. Just pick your confidants carefully and prayerfully.

Book knowledge or second-hand knowledge is adequate when that is all you have to offer, but sharing of life experiences will bring authenticity to your ministry. Often your greatest gift of ministry may be to connect a person of faith who has survived a similar life tragedy with the person who is in the midst of the storm. Remember that "perfect" people do not make good ministers. We all are imperfect and dependent on the grace of God to make "lemonade out of lemons." So when you have survived "hard times," ask yourself and God, "What can I learn about myself and God from this experience, and how can I use what I have learned to help others?"

Professional Dress and Demeanor

Part of "being your best" as a minister is your packaging. There seems to be a new trend toward "casual" appearance. We don't need to overdress, but we need to give careful attention to our appearance. People may judge the content of our ministry initially by their first impression, which is usually visual. Marketing has never been more important than it is in today's world. People buy food, cars, houses, vacation Bible school literature, and many other items based on their packaging. We are cautioned to be wise consumers and not judge a book by its cover, but covers still sell books, and people still initially judge people by the way they look. Take a look at yourself and ask if your appearance accurately reflects what is inside. Does your appearance invite others to relate to you? Does your appearance "match" your ministry field? You need to dress as the majority of your adult parishioners dress if you want to be taken seriously.

A graphic artist once observed that you can have a wonderful conference, but if the quality of the promotion does not encourage them to attend, many people will not benefit from the content of the conference. Likewise, if your appearance is off putting to people, many of them may not benefit from the content of your ministry. Fashion is not a priority for some people, but your general appearance needs to invite people, both children and adults, to relate to you, listen to you, and take your ministry seriously because you are the vehicle by which many will come to know God personally. When you dress professionally, you might also include something that is inviting–a pin, a tie, a vest, earrings, or something else that draws children and adults who love children to you. That doesn't mean that you dress childishly or even humorously. It means you dress to attract children and their parents.

A critical dimension of your appearance is your demeanor. Does your demeanor, your attitude about life, invite people to you? You should be authentic, but few people want to be around a complainer, a criticizer, or a pessimist.

Healthy Minister

A fatigued, run-down, overworked minister is not an effective minister. A church will not take care of your health. Only you know the demands that are made from all directions, because the next person does not know what all of the other previous people have requested that you do today or this week. Most churches will usurp all the time and energy you will allow them, so you must set your own limits to keep yourself physically and mentally healthy. Listen to your body. Take care of the most precious tool of your ministry by eating healthily and exercising adequately as well. To retain mental health ministers must discover the practices that refresh them when they are "bone weary." It may be as simple as a hot bubble bath, listening to favorite music, swimming, hiking, or skiing. It might be a longer event that requires planning and vacation days, such as taking a long trip to an exotic location, visiting friends that live a distance away, going to the beach or mountains, or taking a retreat to a favorite place of solitude.

For mental and physical heath, take your weekly "day off," and never lose yearly vacation days. Help people in your ministry area as well as other staff members to adjust to your schedule, but be flexible if you need to minister in crisis. If we do not pay attention to our mental and physical health, we will not have optimum energy to do the ministry. Then the children, parents, leaders, and other ministers will not benefit from what we could contribute if we were at our best.

When a Church "Calls"

Every church has procedures for securing leaders to guide its preschool and grade-school ministries. Most churches have different systems for paid ministers and volunteer leaders/ministers, although the job descriptions can be very similar. Volunteer leaders or ministers usually are invited into the ministry leadership from the laity. A person who has passion for the ministry as well as demonstrated leadership and relationship skills may be approached about becoming an elected or appointed volunteer leader/minister.

Increasing numbers of churches are tapping people from the congregation to become paid staff leaders/ministers. Some churches prefer to employ someone from outside the church membership. Whether the leader/minister is "called" by the church from within or outside the congregation, and whether he or she is paid or volunteer, information about the church and its expectations will help the minister to discern with God's guidance whether this is a good ministry match. If a minister knows little information about the congregation, he or she might consider asking some of these questions to the person, committee, or team interviewing prospective ministers:

1. What is this church doing best in preschool and grade-school ministry? If parents brought their children to this church for the first time, what would be the reasons they might bring them back?

   These questions will help you to discern what the committee members consider their strengths and perhaps their priorities or values in the ministry. If possible, these questions also need to be asked of parents not in the minister-enlisting process if such an opportunity is presented.

2. What new ministries have you considered beginning? Why?

   Is the congregation "dreaming," or do they simply want someone to help them do what they are already doing? Some churches want someone to do what other churches are doing without consideration as to whether it is truly needed or can be realistically implemented with the church's current resources. However, other churches know that to implement ministries they have assessed as necessary and possible to accomplish their vision, they need someone to guide them in accomplishing that dream.

3. How do the preschool weekday program(s) and/or after-school programs interact with the church programs? How is supervision and coordination of that ministry handled?

   The same rooms and even resources are used by multiple ministries in some churches. Scheduling, room arrangement, and sharing of resources can become a battle if the church does not have a clear supervision of programs. It is important to know if the supervision or directing of the weekday ministries is a part of the position expectations.

4. What would be my role in ministry with parents?

   Some churches have not considered the importance of ministry to parents as a significant part of ministry to their children. Other churches may have another minister assigned that responsibility.

Try to discern if the preschool and grade-school minister would be allowed to work cooperatively with the "family" minister as a part of his or her responsibilities. Use this interview as a time to express your interest and belief in the value of family nurturing.

5. How do you meet the worship needs of preschoolers and grade-schoolers? (children's worship service or "children's church," preschool worship care/teaching, children's sermon, etc.) What would be my role?

Discover whether they address the worship needs of preschoolers and grade-schoolers. Are they inclusive of children in worship? Is there a "children's sermon" as a part of the congregational worship experience? Who delivers it? Do they have a separate children's worship service (sometimes called "children's church") that is conducted concurrently with the adult service? Is there preschool worship care? How are the preschool worship needs addressed in that ministry?

6. What is the practice or process when a child indicates an interest in accepting Jesus as his or her Savior? What would be my role in that process?

While some denominations have confirmation classes for children at a designated age, other faith traditions wait for the child to indicate interest in making a public profession of faith in Jesus and to express a desire to follow his leading in life directions. Whatever the practice of the church, the preschool and grade-school minister needs to be included in that process.

7. For what church programs/ministries would I be directly responsible? Would I be expected to administer the programs or be the leader?

Expectations are often assumed by both the church and the prospective minister. The church may be expecting the minister to be the leader of a program, while the minister expects to be the organizer, trainer, and encourager of the enlisted leader(s). A minister who is the program leader of some or many of the programs will not be able to grow a ministry to the extent one could as the equipper, trainer, and encourager of other leaders. A ministry that is built around one minister will deprive others of the opportunity and joy of ministry. One person has a limited amount of time, so the ministry is limited to what only one person can do. If many people are trained and invited into the joy of ministry, the programming can expand as more leaders are developed.

8. What would be my role (if any) in congregational worship?

Since preschool and grade-school ministers do much of their ministry out of sight of most of the congregation, they often are "unseen," particularly by people who do not have young children. Visibility of the minister and the ministry before the congregation is important to emphasize its contribution to the total ministry of the church. Often, the age group ministers have worship leadership responsibilities on a rotation basis in larger churches and every Sunday in smaller churches. It is also good modeling for children and their parents to see "their minister" leading in prayer, reading Scripture, using musical talents, or even preaching from time to time.

9. How would I relate to the other ministerial staff positions?

It always helps to know who supervises whom. Is every staff position supervised by the pastor, or is the preschool and grade-school minister supervised by another staff minister? Will any other staff positions be under your supervision (i.e., the weekday director, the preschool worship care coordinator, etc.)? Will all staff ministers be included in the weekly or scheduled staff meetings? Understanding the expected role on the church staff will eliminate many surprises after election or employment for a position.

Salary and other Compensation

Dealing with salary and compensation is not especially comfortable for most ministers, but it is important to address after the initial interview. Often in the second interview or in a subsequent conversation with the committee or pastor, the topic of salary needs to be dealt with. If they do not address it, you will need to bring it up yourself. Be familiar with what comparable professionals in the church community are paid. They may not be childhood ministers, but salaries of school teachers with equal education and experience can indicate a fair salary range. Also note the salaries of the other staff if that information is available. If all of the salaries are lumped together, as they often are, indicate to the committee that you expect comparable compensation.

In addition to your base salary, ask about and/or negotiate for health insurance, reimbursement for business expenses and conferences for continuing education, contributions to retirement funds, book allowance, and a study leave agreement. You may not be given all of that, but if you ask, you might discover a generous congregation.

So to What Are You Called?

More than anything else, you are called to first be a surrendering, obedient child of God, and then to be a minister who reflects the passion and compassion of the Savior to preschoolers, grade-schoolers, parents, teachers and leaders, other ministers, and anyone else God places in your life.

CHAPTER 14

What Does the Church Need to Consider in Calling/Hiring a Preschool and/or Grade-school Minister/Leader?

The number of churches adding a ministry position for preschool and grade-school children and their families has risen significantly. Whether the position is full-time or part-time, paid staff or volunteer, churches recognize that finding the right person to guide this ministry is crucial to their relevance to today's culture. In addition, brain research and faith formation research is underlining the impact of formative childhood years to the mature faith of future church leaders.

For many churches, this is a new ministry leadership venture. While some churches know what they want and what to look for, most churches would like some guidance in making this "young" ministry venture a successful and productive one. Many churches form committees, sometimes called "search committees" or "search teams," to find a person to recommend to the church as this minister (leader, director, or other preferred title). Sometimes a church will use existing groups such as a Preschool and/or Grade-school Ministry Team or personnel committee to look for this new minister. Often they need guidance in the process of developing a ministry job description as well as locating and interviewing prospective candidates.

Developing a Job (Ministry Position) Description and Minister/Leader Profile

Develop a job or ministry position description so that the expectations of the minister will be clear. What do you expect this person to do in this ministry? Will there be some flexibility, depending on his or her unique gifts and abilities?

Consider including in your job or position description the following (see appendix 5 for samples):

- Supervision (by whom as well as of whom)
- Hours expected per week or month (if part-time or hourly position)

- Specific ages of preschoolers and grade-schoolers included in ministry
- Programs included in ministry
- Responsibilities related to securing and equipping of leadership for ministry (It is strongly recommended that this minister have input into all programming related to preschoolers and grade-schoolers and that he or she be an enlister and equipper of leaders rather than a program leader or, even worse, a children's activities director.)
- Family ministry responsibilities
- Other church responsibilities such as worship leadership, committee liaison expectations, etc.

Develop a profile of the minister who would be the ideal candidate, but prioritize the items since you seldom find a minister that will meet all of your desired criteria. Here are some criteria you might include:

- Relates well to preschoolers and grade-school children
- Relates well to adults (parents, leaders)
- Sees him- or herself as a minister, not as an activities director
- Is a good team player on staff
- Can see the big ministry picture for the church and is not solely focused on his or her ministry; can coordinate well with other ministers and ministries
- Can advocate for ministry as well as educate staff and church when appropriate
- Understands faith development of preschoolers and grade-school children and is willing to counsel and grow children as well as assist parents in their responsibilities
- Is comfortable with public ministerial duties such as worship leadership, etc.
- Is knowledgeable in both preschool and grade-schoolers ministry either through education or considerable experience (You can be more specific and list a preference for education degrees or years of ministry-related experience desired if it is an important criterion for your church.)
- Conducts himself or herself in a professional manner

Here are some things you may not know but need to consider:

- Hours for a part-time minister are seldom enough to accomplish what most churches expect.
- Preschool and grade-school ministry is labor intensive. Most of the work of enlisting, scheduling, purchasing, etc., is done out of the sight of almost everyone. Every time a church organization holds an event, childcare is always expected, especially for preschoolers. While adults are in worship, preschoolers need care/teaching, and sometimes you

have to staff a grade-school worship service as well. This minister is often responsible for the supplies, equipment, and sanitation of toys and furniture for every activity. The appropriate teacher/child ratio is quite low for children, so many leaders must be enlisted. If someone doesn't show up to teach, a substitute must be secured, unlike in adult groups, which may be combined or led by one of those in attendance.

- Demand is higher than the supply of trained or experienced ministers in this area of ministry. Many churches are "calling out" leaders from within their membership to receive training or mentoring even while they begin the ministry position. Usually they are already committed to the vision of the church, have been involved in the ministry to preschoolers and/or grade-schoolers, have the respect of and relationships with people to make the transition to church staff or "official leader," and agree to specific personal educational experiences, usually a stipulation for hiring/calling them.

Interviewing Prospective Ministers

When the top candidates have been identified for an initial interview, inform them of the process that will be followed. Some committees deal with only one prospective minister at a time. Others have initial interviews with several ministers, then choose one to pursue further. Let them know when you will inform them of the results of the interviews. If the process ends with someone's initial interview, let that person know in a timely manner. If a person is selected to continue with the process through additional interviews, visits, or discussions, let him or her know that as well.

In an interview, ask questions in the form of what they have done in the past in similar situations rather than what they might do. Some of the questions you might ask are the following:

- What do you most enjoy doing in preschool and grade-school children's ministry?
- What have you done best in preschool and grade-school children's ministry? What do you consider your greatest contribution?
- What new ministries have you begun? What innovative ministries have you begun?
- How have you enlisted and nurtured leadership for preschool and grade-school ministries? Is that difficult for you, or do you enjoy it?
- What process and role do you prefer when a child indicates an interest in accepting Jesus as his or her Savior?
- What experience have you had in weekday preschool ministry? What experience have you had in supervising staff? (*if applicable*)
- What have you done in ministry with parents?

- When a parent or teacher has been upset about something that has happened in the church ministry, what have you done?
- How have you helped to meet the worship needs of preschoolers and grade-schoolers? How would you like to help us to meet the worship needs of our children?
- How do you see preschool and grade-school ministry relating to the other church ministries?
- How have you worked with other staff ministers in other churches? (*If new to church ministry*: How have you related to coworkers in other working relationships?)
- In what congregational worship roles are you most gifted?

Testing the Waters

In addition to interviews during which the committee assesses whether the gifts, abilities, knowledge, and experience are a good match for the expectations of the church, observing the candidate during a visit can be very helpful. Provide several "relaxed" opportunities to interact with a variety of people. Observe his or her ability to relate to all ages of preschool and grade-school children. The candidate may not be a "pied piper," but he or she should be able to engage most of the children even if a little limited because of being a stranger. The candidate should show genuine interest in and respect for the youngsters.

Give him or her occasions to interact with parents, too. Does the candidate seem comfortable and engaged in meeting new people? Hopefully, he or she will be meeting new families that come to your church, and he or she needs to be able to be inviting in demeanor. Especially if the candidate is not already in the church, give him or her opportunities to relate to teachers/leaders. Does the prospective minister seem to elicit respect and project a caring interest in the leadership?

What Are They Worth?

Salary must be offered and accepted as adequate compensation for the work performed. What you offer a potential minister may be set by the church and have little negotiation potential. The range of salaries for the same position even in comparable churches is huge. If there is an opportunity to have input into the salary amount, consider some of these factors:

- Number of people involved in the ministry—preschoolers and grade-schoolers, parents, teachers/leaders (this is often a considerably larger number of people than any of the other age group ministries)
- Number of hours minister is expected to work (be realistic)
- Cost of living in your community

- Salaries of comparable professionals in community (school teachers, childcare directors, etc.)
- Education of minister
- Experience of minister

While most ministers are not focused on monetary compensation, even Jesus said, "A workman is worthy of his hire." We want our ministers to feel valued and appreciated rather than used and mistreated. Make sure that comparable positions are treated equitably as well when it comes to benefits. In addition to base salary, ministers often receive compensation for health insurance, reimbursement for business expenses and conferences for continuing education, contributions to retirement funds, and some churches provide book allowance and study leave agreements.

A Word about Combination Ministries

Some churches are combining ministry positions in an effort to have one full-time position rather than two part-time positions. A number of churches have unrelated combinations such as "Minister of Youth and Children" or "Minister of Music and Children." A church must recognize that these combination ministry positions require different skill sets for each part of the ministry. A good Minister to Youth is not often an effective Minister to Children. Too often a church gets one or the other ministry strength, and the nonskilled area of ministry suffers.

A church is often better served by two part-time ministry leaders rather than one full-time minister if the part-time ministers have passion and skill in their appropriate ministry area. Another option is to require additional education/training in the portion of the ministry position for which the combination minister has the least preparation. As a rule of thumb, carefully consider if a combined ministry position is your best option and, if it is, commit to helping the minister be successful through training, mentoring, or perhaps a volunteer assistant with strengths in the minister's weakest area.

CHAPTER 15

How Do You Learn What You Are to Do as a Preschool and/or Grade-school Minister?

Thirty years ago only a few churches had childhood ministers. These were predominantly large urban churches. Other churches had committed volunteer directors who coordinated the ministry, but they mostly ensured that the children had a teacher, literature, and expendable supplies. The children's ministers that were paid staff were most often trained in a seminary or Christian college. The majority were women, often single women, although some of them married in seminary and became excellent volunteer ministers in the churches where their husbands served as pastors or staff ministers.

As more churches of all sizes have begun to add preschool and grade-school children's ministers to their staff, a shortage of capable, knowledgeable ministers has developed, especially ministers with training to fulfill the churches' ministry expectations. Even most seminary or divinity school graduates today have little preparation for childhood ministry since seminaries rarely offer courses focused on that age group. More and more of the larger seminaries are seeking to fill this void.

Increasing numbers of churches are exercising a new pattern of identifying committed leaders from the laity and inviting them to serve on the church staff. The advantage of utilizing such a person is that he or she already is committed to the vision and mission of the church and often stays in the position longer than those who are employed from outside the congregation. Congregation members "called" to ministry often know the people involved in the ministry—preschoolers, grade-schoolers, parents, and leadership—and already have respect as volunteer leaders.

Often the surprise that strikes without warning, especially to the new minister, is the major shift that occurs when a volunteer leader becomes a paid staff minister. The expectations change, and the relationships change. It isn't simply a matter of getting paid for what he or she might have been doing already in the ministry; the expectation of the congregation is that it will be better than it was before. To become better equipped to lead this specialized age group ministry, ministers are looking for options for learning and growing.

Classroom Options

Basic child development courses can be taken through community colleges as well as colleges and universities. If the minister does not have a child development background, that information will be helpful in understanding how to minister to and teach the different age groups, although there rarely is assistance with faith development unless one attends a private Christian college.

We have more seminaries and divinity schools located around the country than ever before. Many of the larger schools even have satellite campuses in other locations. Increasingly, on-line courses of study are offered for credit through these institutions as well. However, few seminaries or divinity schools offer specialized courses or even substantial parts of general courses for childhood education.

A newer classroom option is a certificate program both for ministers who have college degrees and those who do not. Some seminaries and divinity schools offer certificate courses with a preschool and grade-school ministry focus as part of their degree programs. They vary in format and schedule, depending on the institution offering the certification, but they are frequently taught in concentrated format rather than weekly format for ministers who cannot travel to a "campus class" weekly because of distance.

Many ministers are students as well and receive their degree or certification with their church's support. Not only does the church allow the minister to use work hours to attend the courses, but they also pay for the courses, especially if they are a condition or expectation of the minister's employment.

Conferences

Conference opportunities are abundant. The challenge is selecting the ones that will be the most helpful in your ministry setting. Conferences are conducted almost any time of the year by publishers of literature, "teaching" churches, denominational agencies, Christian bookstores, independent Christian consultants, and other Christian organizations. Not all of them are helpful to everyone, so be selective of the ones that seem to offer the help needed most. Ask other ministers which ones they have attended that have been most helpful to them in their ministry.

Mentoring

A minister may choose a mentor who is an experienced childhood minister with an effective ministry. The mentor may not come from the largest church or have the most activities. Look for one who seems to be making a difference in the lives of the preschoolers, grade-schoolers, and parents, as well as impacting the ministry of the church in the community. Choose a mentor who relates well to the church staff too.

A one-on-one mentoring relationship can occur over the telephone or through e-mail as well as face-to-face. Sometimes a question can be answered quickly, but sometimes the issue is more of a process that will require substantial consultation and discussion. While a mentor is chosen by the minister desiring to learn from that mentor, the mentor must agree to serve in that role. It takes time, so even if the mentor agrees to guide the new minister, time limits will need to be negotiated at the beginning and perhaps throughout the relationship.

Mentoring also can occur as a minister participates in a group that meets regularly for support and sharing of ideas and resources. Some locations have city or regional organizations, but any group of childhood or age group ministers can agree on a time and location for regular group meetings around a meal or any other time that is convenient for most. In some cases, you may want to relate to a series of mentors who have exceptional gifts in different arenas of ministry. As you learn from other ministers, you will include new elements in the flavor and direction of your unique ministry.

Coaching

Coaching is different from mentoring in that the coach shares little information but instead helps the minister decide on actions to reach his or her desired outcomes. The coach may or may not be a childhood minister or even a minister at all, even though there is a growing network of Christian coaches. For best results, select a coach trained in coaching techniques.

The assumption of coaching is that the person being coached knows his or her setting and parishioners, and can discover the plan of action that will fit his or her situation best. A minister can be coached toward actions such as the following:

- Personal time management
- A ministerial education or continuing education plan
- Reorganization of a ministry
- A relationship challenge
- Communication issues
- A ministry plan

Any phase of ministry that presents a dilemma can be clarified and broken down into action steps through coaching.

Independent Study

Many helpful books can add to your knowledge of preschool and grade-school child development, family ministry, parenting issues, faith formation, cultural trends, and emerging research about the best faith practices in childhood ministry. In addition, magazines and Internet articles from reputable sources can keep you learning for a lifetime. Consider beginning by securing and reading the books in appendix 6.

CHAPTER 16

Where Do You Begin in a Childhood Ministry?

When a childhood minister begins a new ministry, whether it is a first ministry position or a new congregation for an experienced minister, the tendency is to begin making improvements almost immediately. A wiser path is to slowly construct a plan with input and ownership of key leaders and then start slowly building the kind of ministry that you and the church eventually want to have.

It's All about Relationships

People are more likely to follow ministers with whom they have a positive relationship. If you have been a part of the congregation before becoming a minister or director, you will have a relationship base on which to build. It still would be prudent to take some time to experience the relationships from the new role as minister/leader, even if it is a volunteer position. If you are coming to the church without having a relationship with the members of the congregation, the first focus of your new ministry is to build relationships with key groups.

Developing relationships with preschoolers and grade-schoolers

The preschoolers and grade-schoolers in the church need to begin to relate to "their minister" as a friend who likes them and believes in them. They need to feel that you are a person to whom they can turn in any situation. Developing that trust will take time and interaction with both groups as well as individuals. Preschool children need to see their minister in their hallway and rooms as they come to church and as they depart. As you consistently greet them, call them by name, and begin to win their trust, they will begin to initiate contact with you. Spend some time in their program sessions, being careful not to disrupt the planned learning experiences, but rather enhancing it through conversation, music, or appropriate interaction during their activity centers.

Grade-school children also like to be greeted by name and to be known by their minister. Children know if you genuinely care for them and they will respond to your friendly conversation when they become comfortable.

Some will respond immediately; others will take longer. It is not as easy to flow in and out of a grade-school teaching session at church, so substituting for absent teachers once in a while will strengthen your knowledge and relationship with the children.

In addition to relationship building at church, additional strategies can accelerate the breadth and depth of knowledge about the children and their parent(s). Home visits over a period of several months will yield a wealth of information about the families as well as delight the preschoolers and grade-schoolers, who feel especially important since their minister visited their home. Make an appointment for each visit. Keep the time for the visit brief—no longer than thirty minutes unless they detain you. Be sure to spend time with the children as well as the parent(s) or guardian. Visiting in homes is very time consuming, but the value will be immeasurable in building relationships.

Visits to the children's schools (as security will allow), sports events, and recitals will help develop relationships with not only the "church children" but also their friends. Showing an interest in their everyday lives in addition to their church experiences will speed up their confidence in their association with you. Some schools will allow you to eat lunch with the children, but others may not. Almost anyone can attend sports events in which children are involved, but you will need to discover which sports and which children play on the teams.

If your church has a weekday preschool or after-school ministry, you can be present frequently for arrival and departure times. If you are the director of either or both programs, spend some time in the classrooms, interacting with the children and teachers. As you develop relationships with the preschoolers and grade-schoolers, you will discover so much information that you might consider keeping a notebook of information. Some churches have a data base with basic family information to which you could simply add the "extra" items, such as sports played on teams, activities requiring recitals or end-of-year performances, etc. You might prefer to interview children and parents to discover their interests, schedules, vocations and avocations, schools, birthdays, etc., and write these in the notebook.

Developing relationships with parents

In addition to home visits, look for ways to establish a trusting relationship with parents. Let them know that you are interested in them, not just in their children. Choose to be present at some of the adult functions at which many of the parents will be in attendance. Send e-mail messages with information about upcoming ministry events or links to helpful articles. Let them know when you "catch" their child doing something helpful or kind. Let the parents know that you are available any time they need to talk with someone, and that it will be held in strictest confidence. You might want to have a parent event with some time for socializing and some time for listening to their dreams for preschool and grade-school ministry in the next several years. Note the seminars, workshops, and family events that elicit the most interest and excitement.

Developing relationships with teachers/leaders

Your relationship with the teachers and/or leaders will be crucial to building the church's ministry. You cannot do it alone, so you need to cultivate many volunteers to join you in this ministry. Begin by establishing relationships with the current leadership. Learn their names as quickly as possible, and greet them at the beginning of their ministry responsibility. Thank them for their faithful service to the preschoolers or grade-schoolers. Ask how they are doing personally, and note any matters for which you need to pray or follow up during the week. Provide the resources they need to perform an effective ministry, and encourage them. Write notes and e-mails expressing your appreciation as well as noting creative teaching or strong relationships with the children or an unusual effort.

If the teachers or leaders have urgent needs that have been waiting for "the new minister" to arrive and "handle," listen to their concerns and address them appropriately. Some concerns can be handled immediately, but others will need to be processed. Assure the teachers you have heard them and will do what you can. Another way to build relationships with teachers and leaders is to invite them to your home, perhaps in groups, to have dessert or finger foods and just get acquainted. Of course, you can visit their homes or workplaces, but this will most likely occur over a period of years, not months, since visits will occur one-by-one. If the teachers are also parents, a visit to their homes would be doubly productive in building relationships.

Avoid immediately dismissing any teachers or leaders for the first several months. Identify ineffective or uncommitted teachers and leaders. Attempt to redeem them by offering assistance, materials, training, or whatever is needed to make them successful. Sometimes a long-time teacher will have become dated and ineffective in his or her teaching methods but is loved by the church and sometimes (but not always) by the children in his or her class. Develop a relationship with that teacher, and try subtle (or perhaps obvious) ways to improve his or her teaching success. Sometimes the teacher is not open to changing. Make sure you have the backing of the senior pastor and any other groups with supervisory responsibility before terminating a volunteer.

Developing relationships with staff

It is vitally important for the childhood minister to bond with the general church staff. From the senior pastor to the custodian, each one is important in fulfilling the mission of the church. The ministerial staff needs to be a team with personal relationships that include mutual respect and appreciation for the various aspects of ministry. Spending time together discussing, planning, and evaluating the church ministry is important; but forging relationships is equally significant. Social occasions for staff and their families also can build relationships that will carry the staff through cooperative ministry endeavors as well as inevitable disagreements and negotiations.

The childhood minister needs to believe passionately in the importance of his or her ministry, as should every staff minister. However, ministers with tunnel vision often do not recognize the interrelatedness of all of the ministries to the vision of the church. It is important, therefore, for the staff ministers to express appreciation and mutual respect for each other so that the whole ministry is greater than the sum of the ministry areas. Learn in these early days when to "battle" and when to negotiate. Battle only priority issues, and wait until the relationships are more solid before taking on others. As you develop a ministry team, relationships will carry you through more difficult conflicts.

Developing relationships with the rest of the church

Even those people involved in church but not directly related to the childhood ministry can feel connected to it through relationships, but these are the most difficult to establish in most churches. Faith families need granddaddies, grandmothers, aunts, uncles, and cousins, too. The challenge for the childhood minister is to find ways to relate personally and ministerially to senior adults, single adults with no children in these age groups, and empty nest adult couples. It will require intention and creativity in the midst of developing all of the other relationships that seem more central to the ministry. Ministerial duties such as hospital visitation and leading in elements of the worship service can establish you as a minister and create an interest in the ministry you lead.

Evaluating the State of the Ministry

As you are developing relationships, begin to assess the strengths and weaknesses of the existing childhood ministry. Use Part 1 of this book to evaluate each aspect of the ministry for at least the first three to six months. Written notes will assist you in synthesizing the collected information later. Consider these potential avenues for gathering information:

- Make observations of programs, facilities, policies, and the general attitude of the church toward childhood ministry
- Listen to what parents and leaders are saying about their dreams for the ministry
- Pay attention to the comments of the preschoolers and grade-schoolers, and even the youth who once were a part of the childhood ministry;
- Note what people outside the ministry and the church perceive about the ministry to preschoolers and grade-schoolers

• Invite another childhood minister to visit and make observations

If you can pinpoint minor improvements that will be perceived as positive change rather than disturbance, make them one at a time, weighing their effect before proceeding to the next one. Minor positive improvements will help the church to feel that there is progress while you are assessing the need for more radical changes for the future.

For example, a new volunteer childhood minister observed a very poorly conducted "children's church." She first became involved with the leadership of the children's worship service. Then, after a year or so, she suggested that the children attend the first half of the congregational service that included a children's "sermon." Eventually, with the support of the leadership, parents, and staff, she was able to eliminate the children's worship service, provide a special bulletin, and help the worship leaders and parents to get the children fully involved in the service.

Setting Priorities and Making Changes

After you have observed, listened, and recorded responses, begin to identify the primary strengths of the childhood ministry. What is going well? What is making a difference in the lives of the children and their families? For what is the ministry known in the community? What do parents and age group leadership value? Developing a ministry plan beginning with the strengths is far more effective than starting with the weaknesses.

While most churches want to improve their weaknesses, if the energy is expended on the weak points, the strengths will suffer. It is preferable to make the strengths even stronger while developing additional leadership before tackling the weakest areas. Of course, some safety and security lapses may need immediate attention for the welfare of the children; but, in general, highlighting the strengths is an effective strategy.

Occasionally, churches do not deal with changes that should have been made previously. Perhaps the leadership, the pastor, or some of the parents have waited for the new childhood minister to make the changes. While that is not fair to someone who has not had time to develop relationships that can weather conflict, sometimes the changes must be made fairly soon. In such a scenario, do not make the changes unilaterally. Secure the support of the staff, especially the pastor, the age group ministry team if one is in place, or perhaps a team comprised of key age group leaders specifically organized for this purpose.

A volunteer childhood director, newly selected by her church, encountered resistance from a long-time teacher of a grade-school children's Sunday school class. The parents of the children in that class expressed their dissatisfaction with the teaching methods being used. The children were complaining and did not want to attend. However, the pastor did not want her to confront the teacher for fear of upsetting the teacher. As the complaints continued for another year, the director requested that the parents complain to the pastor rather than her. In a short time, the pastor requested that the director, with his support and blessing, talk with the teacher and insist on training in updated teaching methods or another teacher would be enlisted to teach that class. The teacher was given two acceptable choices for the good of the ministry, and the choice was hers.

You can't do everything that needs to be done at once, so—with input from the childhood ministry team or committee—determine the ministry action priorities. What can be done first to have the greatest impact? It may not be the biggest change, but it might make a significant difference.

Here are some examples of small changes:

- Organizing a clean-up day to throw out accumulated "junk" and reorganize teaching materials (a great relationship building experience as well)
- Restocking a resource closet or setting up a resource room for the teachers with basic supplies on hand (this can be expanded as a major priority)
- Getting the hallway floors cleaned (and waxed if they are not carpeted)
- Supplying teachers and/or parents with articles from the Internet or magazines "to think about"
- Sending birthday cards to preschoolers, grade-schoolers, and their teachers (electronic cards are fun to receive, too—look for the free ones!)
- Providing attractive signs for rooms that indicate the ages and programs assigned to that room (moving classes or reorganizing the class age groups would be a major change)

Prioritize the changes that need to be made. Evaluate the impact and disruption each of them could create. Be sure to get input and assessment from the church staff, especially those whose ministries will be affected by the proposed changes or improvements. Seek the wisdom of the experienced staff who know the parishioners and may be able to steer you around the known "landmines." After the ministry priorities have been determined, begin determining the steps to implement them, including a time line and possible communication strategies. Most major changes happen one step at a time, but sometimes they need to take place simultaneously. For example, expanding from one Bible study hour to two Bible study hours on a Sunday morning cannot occur in steps. There are many steps in the change that must be identified and made, but when the change occurs, it happens all at once.

The general wisdom is to make changes at the pace that the congregation can handle them. For many churches it will be slower than the minister would like. For others change is welcomed and embraced. Be a leader, but don't get so far ahead that you lose your followers.

CHAPTER 17

What Are the Roles of a Childhood Minister or Coordinator?

A childhood minister or coordinator is never bored if he or she likes variety. Every day is different, but too often you seem to have little control over how the time is spent. Part-time coordinators struggle constantly with limited time. Even the best-planned days can be preempted with ministry demands from a range of sources, from the senior pastor to the minister's own family. Ministers or coordinators do not have the privilege of doing only what they like to do or even what they are gifted to do. In most childhood ministry positions, several basic roles are usually included in the volunteer or paid minister's responsibilities and must be accomplished by some means.

Refer to Part 1 of this book for specifics in how to accomplish these roles.

Administrator

If administration is your spiritual gift, you will thrive in this position role. If you do not like administrative tasks, hire a secretary or an assistant, or discover some willing volunteers who are gifted in organizing, because childhood ministry is heavily administrative. Some churches value administrative skills above all others, while other churches tolerate a more flexible administrative style.

Administration will be needed for various responsibilities:

- Implementing and maintaining policies and procedures for safety, security, and hygiene
- Keeping records and/or data bases of children, families, and teachers
- Ordering and organizing supplies and teaching resources needed by the volunteer teachers
- Scheduling childcare for church events
- Coordinating worship care for preschoolers and/or children's worship service for grade-schoolers
- Making plans for all programs—teacher/leader enlistment, room assignments, time slots, etc.
- Securing supplies and teaching materials

- Selecting and purchasing literature for all programs
- Determining job descriptions for all teaching and other leadership positions
- Leading in annual and monthly planning with a team
- Maintaining a calendar of activities that coordinates with the church calendar
- Determining the overall priorities of childhood ministry
- Coordinating special activities for preschoolers, grade-schoolers, and families
- Managing a budget
- Conducting other administrative responsibilities that may be unique to your church or position description

A substantial amount of time is occupied with administrative duties, but a minister can delegate many of the details of administration as long as he or she guides, empowers, and supports those to whom the duties were delegated. Delegation is a limitation for many childhood ministers as they tend to be "doers." Often churches expect them to "do" the work rather than empower others to participate in a faith community effort. A childhood minister—especially the part-time or volunteer coordinator/director—who takes it upon him- or herself to do all of the administrative duties will find little time left for the other roles. Find people in the congregation who have the gift of administration and delegate details to them. Whenever the minister does all of the work alone, someone else is deprived of the opportunity of using their gifts and passions in serving God and the children.

When you delegate, keep the difficult or volatile duties for yourself. It isn't fair to give a volunteer an assignment that has high emotion attached to it or is just something you do not want to handle. For example, securing childcare for a Christmas Eve service may not be a good task to delegate since few people want to miss the Christmas Eve service to do childcare; however, the general scheduling of volunteers to work in worship care with preschoolers is a task that can be delegated provided the minister provides support, encouragement, and suggestions. The minister must always be willing to step in when the volunteer needs assistance or cannot complete the assignment. Remember that not everyone will complete a delegated assignment as you would complete it. Often, however, others will have a better idea or at least a comparable one. Reserve the right to veto any inappropriate procedures, but try to redeem the situation to make it a successful experience.

Budgeting is a very important administrative duty that you will not delegate. Many churches will elect a volunteer childhood coordinator but provide inadequate budget money for the ministry. Other churches designate budget money for a part-time or full-time minister but fail to add adequate budget to support the ministry. One of the first administrative responsibilities is to evaluate the cost of the ministry, especially the priorities that you have identified in the first 6–12 months. If the budget is inadequate (and it often is), create an itemized budget for the next year, outlining in detail your request and how it will be designated for each priority. Do your homework. Be prepared to advocate for each priority, justifying the cost that you are requesting.

Planning is a vital and constant administrative responsibility that will be accomplished sometimes on your own, sometimes with a planning team, and other times through delegation. Annual planning is a ministry team endeavor (see chapters 1 and 11). Planning for the organizations or programs will most likely begin as a solitary effort that will eventually expand to include program leadership. Teaching sessions as well as special events will primarily be planned by the responsible teachers or leaders. Inadequate planning will create uncertainty, frustration, dissatisfaction, and confusion in a ministry. Thorough planning, on the other hand, will communicate the importance and attention that is being given to the ministry and to those involved in the ministry. Make sure that you are planning adequately, and then stress the importance of planning to program leaders as well as teachers.

Enlistment is another administrative responsibility that in most churches is a constant in preschool and grade-school ministry. Many teachers/leaders are needed for these age groups because of low appropriate teacher to pupil ratios, as well as the number of programs and childcare events the church provides. Then there are the teachers or leaders who will serve for only "a term" or work on a team event before they return to their adult classes. Rarely does a church have an adequate number of leaders. A waiting list is a dream! The result is year-round enlistment for either long-term or short-term service. Enlistment guidelines are given in chapter 4.

Check with other ministers, especially childhood ministers, to discover administrative "systems" or ways of getting the responsibilities done. Experienced childhood ministers usually are delighted to share administrative techniques they have developed over many years.

Educator

God does not always call the people who know the most to be ministers. However, God does expect his willing, committed leaders to prepare themselves to be the most effective leaders they can be. An educator must be a learner as well, assessing areas in which knowledge and/or experience are needed to inform and lead others. Often childhood ministers become frustrated when others do not understand the issues, approaches, or concerns that they are trying to convey. The childhood minister may first need to educate others because often the problem is that "they don't know what they don't know." When you meet resistance or even hesitancy in following your lead, consider that you may need to pause for some learning to take place rather than "pushing it through."

The childhood minister is responsible for the education of

- preschoolers and grade-schoolers (as a supplement to their parents' instruction)
- parents and/or guardians
- teachers/leaders of the various programs
- other ministers on the church staff
- the congregation in general
- the community (as an advocate for issues related to preschoolers and grade-schoolers)

Some common areas that frequently require instruction through discussion or training sessions are the following:

- preschool and grade-school child development—the typical physical, mental, emotional, and social growth patterns that emerge or unfold at various ages
- learning styles of children that affect the way they learn most successfully
- effective teaching methods that maximize learning
- faith formation process that informs the way parents and teachers guide preschoolers and grade-schoolers in knowing and experiencing God
- worship needs and contributions of children to the worshiping faith community
- counseling a child about conversion in ways and at times the Holy Spirit is working in his or her life
- literature selection that meets the vision and teaching goals of the congregation
- protection of minors from predators (even at church)
- safety concerns for the protection of preschoolers and grade-schoolers while they are at church
- accomplishing the parental role in the faith nurturing of children

The educator responsibility is one of the most important roles in growing a ministry, but it can become "lost in the ministry details" unless a minister values its impact. At first you may feel as if you are the sole voice in "standing up for the children." Your ultimate goal as educator is to develop leaders, not followers. Use the example of Jesus. A superb leader, when his earthly ministry was completed and the Holy Spirit came, the disciples were ready to be leaders, not followers. You will know you are being a successful educator when you hear others advocating for what is best for the children.

Equipper and Nurturer

Enlistment of the volunteers in the childhood ministry is only the beginning of the minister's responsibility to the leadership. While excellent enlistment methods are a good start, equipping and nurturing leadership will grow them into good childhood leaders and will retain them longer. One of your goals is to reduce the turnover that repeatedly occurs in childhood ministry because of lack of support or encouragement that causes burn-out. Limit the number of program leadership responsibilities so that they can have adult church experiences, too. Refer to Part 1, chapter 4, for details about equipping and nurturing teachers.

Others in the childhood ministry will need equipping and nurturing as well. Parents will need encouragement, and many moms and dads will seek assistance in rearing their children. The childhood minister must be prepared with recommended resources or be willing to search for assistance. A parent library with print media and multimedia resources would be extremely helpful for general parenting topics. See Part 1, chapter 3, for ways the ministry can equip parents.

Communicator

A childhood minister must be willing and able to clearly converse about the age group ministry. You must be motivated to "tell the story" of childhood ministry and the difference it is making in your families and congregation. See Part 1, chapter 7, for specific information.

All communication needs to be done well. In our consumer-driven, slick advertising society, typographical errors, incorrect information, and grammatical errors in written communication are perceived as second-rate. You must make sure that your communications are proofread for accuracy and visually attractive or appealing to the audience you are trying to reach because the quality of the communication is perceived as the quality of the ministry.

Curriculum Developer

Curriculum for ministry includes the overall design of what you want to teach children. The content of the curriculum can be published literature that accomplishes your desired curriculum. It may be adapted from printed literature, or it may be written specifically for your church, even by you or your leadership. For example, you and/or your leadership team may determine that you want a curriculum that includes the following:

- *Bible study and Bible skill development*—content specific for various ages
- *Discipleship*—spiritual discipline studies (prayer, Bible reading, stewardship, missions, etc.) as well as discipleship experiences
- *Worship*—teaching about worship and worship services, as well as providing worship experiences

- *Community*–interaction with other people of faith, both age mates and other generations
- *Ministry*–opportunities for children to experience ministry and provide ministry perhaps through missions education and action
- *Evangelism*–a plan for laying foundations for a personal relationship with Jesus Christ as well as inquirers' instruction and a process for guiding conversion decisions
- *Music*–teaching biblical concepts through musical experiences, worship participation through musical experiences (such as a choir or praise team as well as congregational singing), and music instruction

The childhood ministry curriculum must have balance, much like the nutritious balance in a child's diet. You will need to insure that the children are getting all of the elements of the determined curriculum as a part of their regular programming. While some programs emphasize Bible study or verse memorization, others will concentrate on discipleship, worship, or music, for example.

Be careful to avoid instituting popular programs that may be successful in other churches but if begun in your church would be repetitive of another program's purpose as well as eliminate one of your valued curriculum elements. The author was consulting with a childhood ministry planning team in a small-town church. In listing the programs they were doing well in their ministry, as well as the curriculum elements they valued, I noted that they expressed a desire for the children to participate in mission experiences, a ministry highly valued by the youth and adults of the church. Yet they had recently replaced their mission education program with an additional discipleship program that included a new, popular, and heavily promoted literature. They had to rethink what they valued and how they were going to incorporate those values with their ministry to preschoolers and grade-schoolers in a balanced curriculum.

Once a church determines the ministry curriculum that it will include for the faith development for its preschoolers and grade-schoolers, it is ready to select the literature or write the literature that accomplishes the desired curriculum. See Part 1, chapter 11, for more information about literature selection guidelines.

Caregiver

An endearing role for a childhood minister is that of caregiver. Children, parents, and teachers or leaders can be the object of care. When children are sick, hurt, or dealing with a crisis situation, the childhood minister needs to be "present" for the child. Often the parents are overwhelmed by the events, so a support system from outside the family can be of valuable assistance and encouragement. Teachers need to know that you care about them, too, not just what they can do for the ministry.

Childhood ministers need to be sensitive to ministry to a child and his or her family during stressful events such as the following:

- Hospitalization of child
- Divorce of parents
- Remarriage of a parent or becoming a member of a blended family;
- Child illness at home
- Serious illness of a paren
- Death of a pet
- Death of a family member, including a grandparent
- Unemployment of parent
- Deployment of a parent in a branch of military service
- Birth of a sibling
- Moving to a new home, school, or city
- Parent addiction to drugs or alcohol

How you provide care is not as important as being present for the child, parent, or teacher. You may not know what to say, but demonstrating that you care about them will be remembered for a lifetime. Here are some ways that you might be a caregiver:

- Visit the hospital or home for a short call
- Notes of encouragement (children love to get mail)
- Take over a gift such as a book or a gift certificate to a favorite fast-food restaurant
- Take the child out to eat a favorite food or dessert
- Go to a park to play
- Attend memorial services of family members
- Organize meals to take to the home if needed or if it would be helpful
- Call to check periodically on the situation
- Offer to refer for professional counseling services
- Offer financial assistance from the church benevolence fund if appropriate
- Other acts of kindness and care that seem suitable for the situation

The author's biggest surprise in my first ministry position was the number of parents that came to my office for counseling. I was young and did not have children, so I was taken aback that they were coming to me. They would ask about whether certain childhood behaviors were normal (and most of the time they were), possible solutions for problems they were having with their children, discipline or behavior issues and strategies, how to answer faith questions that their children were asking, and even how to do sex education! (That was an interesting one.) What I soon recognized was that I was a new resource that the parents were tapping for information.

They mostly needed someone to suggest a resource or a strategy, or perhaps they were looking for an assurance that they were "on track," or that they might need to make a "course correction." They responded to my involvement in their parenting strategies, and soon I was able to offer targeted seminars that were well attended.

Caregiving during natural or catastrophic disasters

Caregiving might be necessary during and in the aftermath of natural or catastrophic disasters such as tornados, hurricanes, or floods, as well as fire, murders, or terrorists attacks. Ministerial caregiving involves attending to the immediate needs of victims if the disaster occurs in your location. Although the author has been involved in several of the named natural disasters, a more common caregiving responsibility has been to provide support and assistance for children's emotional trauma in the wake of natural disasters.

Children who have experienced a crisis that is sudden are likely to experience psychological shock involving disbelief or numbness, repetitive need to talk about the disaster, fear that is real or imagined, and anxiety—which is unspecified fear. The severity and length of the symptoms depend on the severity of the terror, the degree of surprise, the availability of parents and adult caregivers, the way those adults handle the crisis, and the personality of the child.

Of course, direct survivors are the most seriously affected by a traumatic event, but the indirect survivors also evidence emotional reactions, such as difficulty in sleeping, guilt for having been spared, and sometimes domestic conflict because of the stress of the situation. The childhood minister who is aware of these reactions can be present to reassure and walk alongside both the children and the adult survivors. Children have several basic fears when it comes to traumatic events. Primarily they want to know how this will affect them. They want assurance that the event will not happen again, that they will not be separated from their family, that they will not be left alone, and that more people will not be injured or killed. While we cannot always give them such assurance because we don't know the future, we can help them to understand that this was an unusual event that most likely will not be repeated, although anything is possible. It is best never to lie to a child, but to assure them as much as possible of their safety and security.

When the World Trade Center was attacked on September 11, 2001, many childhood ministers, counselors, and other knowledgeable professionals provided written guidance on the Internet. It was shared far and wide, and parents, teachers, and ministers had excellent assistance for minimizing the depth and length of the trauma that people of all ages experienced, but especially the children. Look for related articles on such topics, and file them away for future use should they be needed.

Caregiving with death experiences

One of the most difficult experiences parents and other adults face with children is death.

Children respond differently depending on their personalities, past experiences with death, the reactions of those around them, their emotional connection to the dead persons or pets, their understanding of the meaning of death, and their ability to verbalize what they are feeling. The childhood minister can be most effective in supporting and guiding parents (if they are emotionally able) to understand and guide their child through dealing with a death. Death threatens a child's security, one of the three basic needs (love, acceptance, and security). Death is always in the context of "what does this mean to my life" and is felt as a danger, either real or imagined.

A child's ability to understand the meaning of death varies with age. A preschooler younger than three years of age seldom understands death except as he or she reflects the emotions of those important in his or her life. From 3–6 years of age, the child also will reflect the feelings, and at the same time he or she will not view death as permanent and final. The child believes that the person will come back even though he or she can tell you what you have said–that the person is dead. Children cannot conceive of their own deaths, but they are often afraid that the important adults in their lives will die (go away). They have little concept of time and live very much in the present. It is important to empathize with their feelings and their lack of understanding of the finality of death. In explaining a death, state the facts that the person is dead and that he or she cannot breathe, eat, play, or be with the child any more.

From 5–9 years of age the finality of death begins to be understood as children age. Five-to-six-year-olds begin to have death anxiety, particularly the death of parents and, later, themselves. They will ask a lot of questions about the details of death as well as the mechanics of body preparation and burial. Their questions need to be answered as honestly as possible. This is how they try to exert some control over their fears. They are fascinated by cause and effect, so they will ask what caused the death, often personifying the cause of death as somebody's fault–maybe theirs. They do believe that their thoughts and actions cause certain results, so they might feel guilty, thinking that they caused the death. It is common for children to be angry with the dead persons for leaving them or not telling them they were leaving.

In later childhood, around 10–12 years of age, children have a more realistic understanding of what is living and what is not living. They also begin to conceive of death as not caused externally but as an internal dysfunction that causes life to end. Of course, violent deaths from accidents or murder are seen as caused externally. Their stage of moral development gives them a strong sense of right and wrong that leads them to the conclusion that sometimes death is punishment for misdeeds. Death is associated with sadness and evil. It is very important at this age for death rituals to be followed, such as burial and funerals.

When the adults understand that children do not perceive death as they do, then they can help children to process the experience in the context of their understanding, knowing that the next death encounter will most likely need to be handled differently because the children will be older and in a different stage of understanding.

Caregiving will involve being sensitive to the stages of grief that the children and/or parents may be experiencing, and assisting them in processing their grief in such a way that they keep progressing through the stages rather than getting caught in an early stage. The stages of grief commonly experienced are denial, anger, bargaining, depression, and acceptance. These stages are expressed in different ways at different ages.

Sometimes grieving children need someone with whom to talk. Every now and then, they need time to work out their grief. Occasionally they need professional counseling to resolve their grief. Caregiving involves being available to guide or assist them in their grief journey.

In an effort to make death easier for children, we say things that are not helpful and may only exacerbate the crisis. Avoid such "explanations" as the following:

- "He/she has gone to sleep." (They will be afraid to go to sleep.)
- "He/she was taken by God." (Will God take me away from my family?)
- "He/she is now an angel." (Humanity and angels are two different creations of God.)
- "God wanted him/her in heaven because he/she was so good." (If I am good, will God take me—I think I will be bad so I can stay with you.)
- "He/she lost his life." (If it's lost, let's look for it.)
- "He/she went away on a long trip." (Why would they leave? Don't they love me? Will they come back? What happens the next time Daddy goes on a business trip?)

Be as honest as you can without scaring them. On the other hand, do not lie to protect them because the dishonesty will have to be explained someday and they may not trust you the next time to tell them the truth. For example, you can say that Grandpa was sick and he died, but will the child may think that the next time he or she is sick, he or she will die, too. Perhaps a better explanation is that Grandpa's body was old and something in it went wrong, and he died.

Whatever your caregiving role, with children or adults, follow their cues as to what they need from you, but always offer prayer and comfort. Be "God in skin" for them.

Minister

As mentioned earlier, whatever your title, and whether you are paid staff or a volunteer, you are a minister to those in the childhood ministry. It is important for the children for you to respect your role as their minister by taking advantage of every opportunity to be ministerial. For example, participate as a worship leader in the congregational worship service if your church will allow it. Lead in prayer, read the Scripture lesson, sing a solo (if you are so gifted) in addition to delivering the children's sermon. Let parents, teachers, and other congregants experience you leading activities that are not directly related to childhood ministry, yet are for the whole body.

If your church allows it, be prepared to baptize children in your ministry if they request it, or lead the parent/child dedication services. Preaching the sermon for a Children's Sunday or another invited occasion can be an opportunity for you to highlight the importance of the ministry to the preschoolers and grade-schoolers. Serving the elements of communion might be another opportunity for you to serve as a minister. If you prefer a background role because of your personality, you need to step out of your comfort zone often for the good of the ministry. Work on public speaking skills and confidence, as you are a role model for the children.

You may find other ministerial duties you can embrace. Hospital visitation that is shared with other staff is often a marvelous way to minister to persons outside of your ministry circle, as well as to those you perhaps know well. One new childhood minister was "on call" for the hospital one weekend when the pastor was away. She had the surprise opportunity of journeying with a family as their elderly mother and grandmother died. The minister was unsure of exactly what to do, but her simple caregiving endeared her to the family, who then asked her to conduct the funeral. Several weeks later the other parent died, and the family requested her presence and ministry because of the relationship that had been established.

General committee liaison assignments may be included in your ministerial responsibilities. Again, this would provide opportunities for connecting with people not usually associated with childhood ministry, and it would afford you input into areas that might enhance your ministry with preschoolers and grade-schoolers.

Evaluator

After your initial evaluation of the ministry conducted in the first year (using Part 1 of this book), you must constantly evaluate everything in the ministry to make sure you are on track, accomplishing what you and/or the childhood ministry team has determined as the priorities for ministry. Periodically, you or the team will need to determine which of your strengths could be even stronger and which items that are average could be raised to a higher level:

- *Content of teaching and learning*–Are preschoolers learning what we have determined they should learn? Are grade-schoolers learning what we have determined they should learn?
- *Process of learning*–Are the preschoolers and grade-schoolers engaged in the learning experiences?
- *Teacher performance*–Are the teachers teaching effectively? Are they prepared for their teaching sessions? Do they feel valued and supported in their responsibilities?
- *Facilities/Space*–What needs to be updated next? Have some safety concerns developed?
- *Curriculum and literature*–Are children missing something in their spiritual diet? Do we need to make other choices to make it more balanced?
- *Organization and ministry*–Do we need to make organizational changes to make the ministry more efficient or effective?
- *Parent support*–Do the parents feel that they are receiving the support they need to be the faith nurturers of their children? What else do they need?
- *Outreach*–Are we reaching children and families in our community? Do we need to do something differently to reach out to children and families in the community?
- *Guiding conversion*–Are we doing what we need to do to help the children to have personal relationships with Christ? Are they being effectively discipled as Christ followers?
- *Ministry visibility*–Does most of the congregation know what is happening in childhood ministry? Is the church known for providing an excellent ministry that forms enduring connections with God and others?

Sample Church Survey
for Childhood Ministry

The following questions can be answered in written survey form, "town meeting" dialogues, or individual interviews (adjust choices to fit your church's ministry):

Family Information

Do you have children in the church's ministry?

❏ No ❏ Yes—ages:_____

Do you have grandchildren in the church's ministry?

❏ No ❏ Yes—ages:_____

Do you hold a leadership position in either a preschool or grade-school program?

❏ No ❏ Yes—ages:_____

1. What do you value most about a church's ministry to preschool and/or grade-school children? Rank the following in order of value to you and your children, with 1 being of the most value:

Preschool (Birth–Kindergarten)

_____ Quality programs (Sunday school, music group, etc.)

_____ Inviting facilities (preschool halls, rooms, playgrounds)

_____ Purposeful teaching rather than babysitting

_____ Caring and attentive leaders/teachers

_____ Cleanliness

_____ Security and safety

_____ Parent seminars, workshops, support groups, etc.

_____ Preparedness for special needs preschoolers

_____ Multigenerational or family activities

_____ Importance of preschool ministry to the whole church

_____ Weekday preschool ministry

_____ Worship care

_____ Other

Grade-school (1–6 Grades)

_____ Quality programs (Sunday school, music/choir, camps, etc.)

_____ Inviting facilities (grade-school halls, rooms, playgrounds)

_____ Purposeful teaching

_____ Caring and attentive leaders/teachers

_____ Cleanliness

_____ Security and safety

_____ Parent seminars, workshops, support groups, etc.

_____ Preparedness for special needs grade-schoolers

_____ Multigenerational or family activities

_____ Importance of grade-school ministry to the whole church

_____ Before- or after-school weekday ministry

_____ Intentional inclusion of grade-schoolers in the congregation's worship service

_____ Children's worship service ("children's church")

_____ Other

2. Which of the above do you think this church does best (list in order)?

1. _____

2. _____

3. _____

3. Which of the above do you think this church needs to pay more attention to?

1. _____

2. _____

4. What do you wish this church would provide for you and/or your children that is not already provided?

1. _____

2. _____

3. _____

Additional comments or suggestions:

Sample Preschool and Grade-school Concepts to Guide Teaching in Church Programs

Basic Concept Categories for Preschool:

1. God	5. Self
2. Jesus	6. Family
3. Natural world	7. Others
4. Bible	8. Church

Basic Concept Categories for Grade-schoolers:

1. Personal acceptance of Christ	5. Christian attitudes and convictions
2. Church membership	6. Christian living
3. Worship	7. Christian service
4. Christian knowledge and understanding	

This is part of a document from First Baptist Church, Raleigh, North Carolina. Used with permission.

Sample Preschool Concept Development

God as Revealed in Jesus		
BIRTH–AGE 2	AGES 2–4	AGES 4–6
a. Associates the words *God* and *Jesus* and phrases such as "God/Jesus loves you" with nurturing caregivers who love him or her. b. Hears songs about God and Jesus. c. Experiences simple stories of God and Bible characters through books read to him or her.	a. Associates *God* and *Jesus* with feelings of love and happiness. b. Begins to learn songs about God and Jesus. c. Experiences moments of awe and wonder when he or she hears that God loves and cares for him or her. d. Begins to ask questions about God and Jesus. e. Thinks of Jesus as a friend who loves and helps him or her. f. Becomes aware of the birth and growth of Jesus. g. Senses wonder about the birth of Jesus.	a. Associates *God* and *Jesus* with feelings of love and happiness. b. Continues to sing songs about God and Jesus. c. Senses that God is always present. d. Knows that God makes and takes care of things in the world. e. Knows that people are dependent upon God and God's provision. f. Feels that God loves him or her, even when he or she does wrong. g. Thanks God for God's love and care. h. Knows that he or she can talk to God at any time and any place. i. Knows that God hears him or her when he or she prays. j. Knows that God showed God's love by sending Jesus. k. Understands that Jesus showed God's love as he grew and as he helped people. l. Knows that God can do miraculous things. m. Knows that God helps him or her in special ways. n. Experiences satisfaction in the everyday world by incorporating the truths that Jesus taught. o. Discovers ways to tell others about Jesus.

Sample Grade-school Concept Development

Personal Acceptance of Christ: God's Forgiveness and Grace		
AGES 6–8	**AGES 8–10**	**AGES 10–12**
a. Child experiences forgiveness from others. Child knows: b. That God loves us and sent God's son, Jesus. c. What it means to forgive. d. That God forgives us when we do wrong. e. That God expects us to forgive others as we have been forgiven.	Child knows that: a. Jesus came to earth and died so that everyone can know the extent of God's love. b. He or she experiences God's grace (forgiveness and power) when he or she asks for it and seeks help to change his or her behavior. c. God's forgiveness heals the damage sin does to his or her relationship with God, but it may not negate the consequences of his or her deeds.	Child understands that: a. God loves us in spite of our sin. b. In Christ's life, death, and resurrection, God has promised forgiveness and fullness of life for every person who repents.

Personal Acceptance of Christ: Nature of Sin		
AGES 6–8	**AGES 8–10**	**AGES 10–12**
Child understands: a. That sin is anything we do or think that separates us from God. b. Some ways to please God. c. That God will help us do what is right.	a. Child has growing understanding of Bible teachings about right and wrong ways to think, feel, and act. b. Child understands that he or she needs God's help to do what is right.	Child understands that: a. All people sin. b. His or her own wrongdoings are sins against God as well as hurtful to self and others.

Personal Acceptance of Christ: Personal Commitment to Christ		
AGES 6–8	AGES 8–10	AGES 10–12
a. Child feels love and reverence for God. b. Child desires to please God. c. Child approaches family and/or appropriate adults for help in understanding Christ. d. Child understands that the Holy Spirit will help the child follow Jesus' teachings about loving God and living with others.	a. Child desires God's forgiveness b. Child understands that a person becomes a Christian by accepting Jesus as the one who restores our relationship with God (Savior) and becomes the ultimate guide for our life (Lord).	a. When led by God's Spirit, the child will make a conscious and personal acceptance of Christ as Lord and Savior.

Parent Guide:
Helping Children to Worship

Speak of attending the worship service as a special opportunity. Help children to anticipate being with their family in a special experience.

Make opportunities for children to talk with worship leaders. Invite them to your home or out to eat so that they will feel that the worship leaders are their friends.

Take care of basic physical needs before the worship service. Take children to the restroom and walk around a little if they have been physically inactive for a while.

Sit together as a family, especially when the children are young. This gives you the ability to guide their behavior as well as to interpret things they may not understand.

Encourage your children to stand and sit with the congregation. They may want to sit during the active part of the service, then stand up when the sermon begins. Not only do they need to participate in the worship experience, but they need the physical movement in order to sit quietly during the sermon.

Involve the children in music experiences. Help them to read the hymnal or projected words. Encourage them to learn the songs. You might sing the songs in the car or at home to help the children become familiar with your church's favorite songs.

Help your children to know how they can best join in prayer. Before worship, discuss concerns or thanks for events or people in the children's lives or your family life. Help them to know they can pray silently while others are praying aloud. Since they have short attention spans, help them to sit quietly if they finish praying before the prayer leader does.

Help your children to find the Scripture passages in their own Bibles. Especially young readers will be eager to find the passages in their Bibles. Use colorful Bible markers to mark the verses ahead of time.

Explain the offering to your children. Let them participate by putting an offering in the plate. Emphasize that it is a way we show love to God. Help them to know where the money goes once it goes in the offering plate.

If your church does not provide children's bulletins, you might want to carry a special worship bag for your children. Include interesting paper, special pencils or markers, and perhaps a book. Children often multitask, listening while they are occupied with an unrelated activity. Change the contents of the bag fairly often.

Help them to listen for certain words, Bible names and places, and other simple concepts. Younger children can draw pictures of things they observe. Older children can keep simple notes.

Prepare them for baptism and communion so they will understand what is occurring. Younger children, who are concrete and literal thinkers, will not understand the symbolic meaning of the ordinances, but they can understand these are important ways for people to remember Jesus and to show others that they are going to follow Jesus' example.

Before and after the service, talk with your children about the invitation time. They may be getting restless by this time. Explain that people are making important decisions about following Jesus during this time, and they need to "practice their patience."

Discuss the service on the way home or after you arrive home, answering questions they may have about the experiences. Ask them what they enjoyed most. Share appropriate thoughts or feelings that you may have had. Keep it short and simple.

Parenting Books

NOTE: There are many other fine books on parenting and family. These are only a few to get your parent library established.

Armstrong, Thomas. *In Their Own Way.* New York: Jeremy P. Tarcher/Putnam, 1987.

Barna, George. *Think Like Jesus.* Ventura, Calif.: Issachar Resources, 2003.

Cartledge, Jan and Tony. *A Whole New World: Life After Bethany.* Macon, Ga: Smyth & Helwys, 2005.

Castleman, Robbie. *Parenting in the Pew.* Downers Grove, Ill.: InterVarsity Press, 1993.

Chapman, Gary, and Ross Campbell. *The Five Love Languages of Children.* Chicago: Northfield, 1997.

Clapp, Rodney. *Families at the Crossroads: Beyond Traditional and Modern Options.* Downers Grove, Ill.: InterVarsity Press, 1993.

Clayton, Lynn P. *10 Gifts Your Children Will Grow to Appreciate.* Macon, Ga.: Peake Road, 1998.

Dockery, Karen. *Growing a Family Where People Really Like Each Other.* Minneapolis Bethany House, 1996.

Elkind, David. *The Hurried Child: Growing Up Too Fast Too Soon.* Reading, Mass.: Perseus Books, 1988.

Fortune, Don and Katie. *Discover Your Children's Gifts.* Grand Rapids, Mich.: Chosen Books, Baker House, 1989.

Fuller, Cheri. *Opening Your Child's Nine Learning Windows.* Grand Rapids, Mich.: Zondervan, 1999.

_____. *Opening Your Child's Spiritual Windows.* Grand Rapids, Mich.: Zondervan, 2001.

Garbarino, James, and Claire Bedard. *Parents Under Siege: Why You Are the Solution, Not the Problem, in Your Child's Life.* New York: The Free Press, 2001.

Garland, Diana R. *Sacred Stories of Ordinary Families: Living the Faith in Daily Life.* San Francisco: Jossey-Bass: 2003. ,

Geary, Thomas and Bonnie. *Nurturing the Souls of Our Children.* Macon, Ga.: Smyth & Helwys, 2002.

Gilbert, Roberta. *Connecting with Our Children.* John Wiley & Sons, 1999.

Habenicht, Donna J. *10 Christian Values Every Kid Should Know.* Hagerstown, Md.: Review and Herald Publishing Association, 2000.

Jones, Timothy. *Nurturing a Child's Soul.* Nashville: Word, 2000.

Lehman, Kevin. *The New Birth Order Book.* Grand Rapids, Mich.: Fleming Revell, 1998.

Morgenthaler, Shirley. *Right from the Start.* St. Louis: Concordia, 2001.

Ng, David, and Virginia Thomas. *Children in the Worshiping Community.* Atlanta: John Knox Press, 1981.

Pipher, Mary. *The Shelter of Each Other: Rebuilding Our Families.* New York: G. P. Putnam's Sons, 1996.

Reeves, Rhonda, compiler. *Tackling Tough Issues.* Birmingham, Ala.: New Hope, 2004.

Sanders, Thomas. *When Can I?* Nashville: Broadman Holman, 2001.

Scott, Jeffery W. *Does Your Child's World Scare You?* Macon, Ga.: Peake Road, 1997.

Smith, Harold Ivan. *When a Child You Love Is Grieving.* Kansas City, Mo.: Beacon Hill Press, 2004.

Stonehouse, Catherine. *Joining Children on the Spiritual Journey.* Grand Rapids, Mich.: BridgePoint Books, Baker Book House, 1998.

Swift, Madelyn. *Getting It Right with Children.* Southlake, Tex.: Stairway Education Programs, 1995.

Swift, Madelyn, and Victoria Mathies. *Teach Your Children Well.* Southlake, Tex.: ChildRight, 2001.

Tobias, Cynthia Ulrich. *Every Child Can Succeed.* Wheaton, Ill.: Tyndale House, 1966.

_____. *You Can't Make Me (But I Can Be Persuaded).* Colorado Springs: Waterbrook Press, 1999.

Trent, John, Rick Osborne, and Kurt Bruner. *Parent's Guide to the Spiritual Growth of Children.* Wheaton, Ill.: Tyndale House, 2000.

Walsh, David. *Selling Out America's Children: How America Puts Profits Before Values— And What Parents Can Do.* Minneapolis: Fairview Press, 1995.

Westerhoff, John H., III. *Will Our Children Have Faith?* Harrisburg, Pa.: Morehouse, 1976.

Wright, Wendy. *Sacred Dwelling: A Spirituality of Family Life.* Leavenworth, Kans.: Forest of Peace, 1994.

Yust, Karen Marie. *Real Kids, Real Faith.* San Francisco: Josey-Bass, 2004

Sample Job Descriptions

Part-time Childhood Minister/Director (Paid or Volunteer)

Responsible To: (Who will be immediate supervisor?)

Number of Hours Per Week (or month): Usually 20–25

General Position Description: To guide in developing and implementing a childhood education ministry (infants through sixth grade) that includes planning, coordinating, and educating.

Ministry Responsibilities:

1. Guide in establishing vision and goals for the childhood ministry.
2. Plan, promote, and guide the religious education programs for pre-schoolers and grade-schoolers such as …(List current ones but leave possibility of adding others).
3. Recruit childhood ministry volunteers and provide them with leadership, resources, and training. (If your church uses a committee to screen and recruit volunteers, outline the role of the minister/director here.)
4. Work with Childhood Ministry Team (or name of coordinating body) in planning programs and activities that meet the needs of children and their parents.
5. Encourage the healthy development of children (spiritually, emotionally, intellectually, physically, and socially) in all aspects of the ministry.
6. Inform children, parents, and church members about children's activities through newsletters, bulletin board displays, e-mail, and announcements.
7. Organize and direct an outreach and visitation program for enlistment and attendance of preschoolers and grade-schoolers.
8. Provide pastoral care and support to children and their parents, including hospital visitation as needed.
9. Provide at least one parenting seminar each year and support parents in their parenting roles throughout the year.
10. Provide and maintain a calendar of activities for preschoolers and grade-schoolers.
11. Assist in worship leadership as requested.

Administration:

1. Attend weekly staff meetings as requested. (Remember this is part-time and may be bi-vocational)
2. Work with other staff in planning activities that will involve the children and families.

3. Prepare a yearly budget for childhood ministry to present to the finance committee.
4. Supervise…(List anyone that will fall under supervision, such as paid childcare workers.)
5. Maintain set office hours for accessibility to children and parents.
6. Perform other tasks as assigned by supervisor when such tasks would enrich and enhance the mission of the church.

This description is not intended as a comprehensive, all-encompassing list of the duties of the Part-time Childhood Minister/Director, but is to serve as a guideline to the responsibilities of the position.

Full-time Childhood Minister/Director (Usually Paid)

Responsible To: (Indicate supervisor–Minister of Education, Associate Pastor, Pastor, etc.)

General Position Description: To assist the church in planning, conducting, promoting, and evaluating a comprehensive and balanced ministry to children (infants through sixth graders) and their families.

Ministerial work as a part of the church's ministerial team

1. Attend regular staff meetings.
2. Participate in worship leadership as requested.
3. Assist with the total visitation program of the church.
4. Participate in hospital visitation and home visits.
5. Provide basic counseling for church members as requested.
6. Be present at all churchwide functions and participate in Sunday and Wednesday programs of worship and education.

Minister to Preschoolers and Grade-schoolers

1. Guide in establishing vision and goals for the childhood ministry.
2. Guide, promote, and administer, in cooperation with the leaders of the childhood programs, the faith education of the church as it relates to preschoolers and grade-schoolers.
3. Work with Childhood Ministry Team (or name of coordinating body) in planning programs and activities that meet the needs of children and their parents.
4. Enlist and equip childhood ministry leadership and provide them with resources and training. (If your church uses a committee to screen and recruit volunteers, outline the role of the minister/director here.)
5. Coordinate planning and presentation of children's sermons with pastor and guide the church in providing worship experiences to meet the needs of children. Work with the pastor in planning parent/child dedication services and assist older preschoolers and their families with introduction to congregational worship.

6. Keep informed about current ministry ideas, resources, and methods in childhood ministry by reading and attending conferences, seminars, and workshops.
7. Evaluate and secure literature, resources, and teaching materials.
8. Develop and implement policies for the safety and security of children.
9. Develop and maintain an active outreach ministry to preschoolers, grade-schoolers, and their families.
10. Plan, organize, staff, and coordinate an effective summer program for children.
11. Provide special events and seminars for parents that will enhance and enrich their parenting skills and relationships with their children.
12. Plan and coordinate special events, fellowships, and ministry opportunities for preschoolers and grade-schoolers.
13. Counsel children and their families about conversion and church membership. (Needs to coincide with church policy.)
14. Supervise the director of the weekday preschool program.
15. Facilitate the sharing of space, resources, and teaching materials by church and childcare teachers.
16. Coordinate and staff the preschool worship care and childcare during special churchwide events.
17. Serve as liaison to… (Name committees or teams to which this staff position will be a liaison.)
18. To develop and administer an annual budget in accordance with the church budgeting process.
19. Perform other tasks as assigned when such tasks would enrich and enhance the mission of the church.

This description is not intended as a comprehensive, all-encompassing list of the duties of the Childhood Minister/Director but is to serve as a guideline to the responsibilities of the position.

Recommended Basic Books for Ministers

Barna, George. *Transforming Children into Spiritual Champions*. Ventura, Calif.: Issachar Resources, 2003.

Beckwith, Ivy. *Postmodern Children's Ministry*. Grand Rapids, Mich.: Youth Specialties/ Zondervan, 2004.

Blazer, Doris A., editor. *Faith Development in Early Childhood*. Kansas City, Mo.: Sheed & Ward, 1989.

Brown, Carolyn C. *You Can Preach to the Kids Too: Designing Sermons for Adults and Children*. Nashville: Abingdon Press, 1997.

Bruce, Barbara. *Our Spiritual Brain: Integrating Brain Research and Faith Development*. Nashville: Abingdon Press, 2002.

Clark, Robert, Joanne Brubaker, and Roy B. Zuck. *Childhood Education in the Church*. Chicago: Moody Press, 1986.

Fowler, James. *Stages of Faith*. New York: HarperCollins, 1981.

Fuller, Cheri. *Opening Your Child's Spiritual Windows*. Grand Rapids, Mich.: Zondervan, 1999.

Gardner, Howard. *Multiple Intelligences*. New York: BasicBooks, 1993.

Jones, Timothy. *Nurturing a Child's Soul*. Nashville: Word, 2000.

Lester, Andrew. *Pastoral Care with Children in Crisis*. Philadelphia: The Westminster Press, 1985.

May, Scottie, Beth Posterski, Catherine Stonehouse, and Linda Cannell. *Children Matter: Celebrating Their Place in the Church, Family, and Community*. Grand Rapids, Mich.: William B. Eerdmans, 2005.

Morgenthaler, Shirley, editor. *Exploring Children's Spiritual Formation: Foundational Issues*. River Forest, Ill.: Pillars Press, 1999.

Ng, David, and Virginia Thomas. *Children in the Worshiping Community*. Atlanta: John Knox Press, 1981.

Ratcliff, Donald. *Handbook of Preschool Religious Education*. Birmingham, Ala.: Religious Education Press, 1988.

_____. *Handbook of Children's Religious Education*. Birmingham, Ala.: Religious Education Press, 1992.

Richards, Lawrence. *Children's Ministry: Nurturing Faith within the Family of God*. Grand Rapids, Mich.: Zondervan, 1983.

Sandell, Elizabeth. *Including Children in Worship: A Planning Guide for Congregations*. Minneapolis: Augsburg Fortress, 1991.

Sims, Suthern. *Creating and Leading Children's Sermons*. Macon, Ga.: Smyth & Helwys, 1999.

Stonehouse, Catherine. *Joining Children on the Spiritual Journey*. Grand Rapids, Mich.: Baker Books, 1998.

Trent, John, Rick Osborne, and Kurt Bruner. *Parent's Guide to the Spiritual Growth of Children*. Wheaton, Ill.: Tyndale House, 2000.

Westerhoff, John H., III. *Will Our Children Have Faith?* Harrisburg, Pa.: Morehouse, 1976.

Yust, Karen Marie. *Real Kids, Real Faith*. San Francisco: Josey-Bass, 2004.

Security and Risk Management Resources

ChurchLawToday.com; 800-222-1840. Paid membership required for e-mail newsletter and online seminars. Extensive legal, tax, and risk management resources for every level of church leadership. Pre-employment screening and background checking service available (ScreenNow and ChoicePoint partnership@www. screenchurchstaff.com.

Nexus Solutions, P.O. Box 165, 3440 Youngfield St., Wheat Ridge, CO 80033; 888-639-8788; www.nexus-solutions.com. Security products include the following:

1. *Good Shepherd Program: Tools to Protect Your Church* by Preventing Child Abuse, $199.95. Includes handbook, model policy manual, background check information, training helps, writable CD of forms, etc. (Some insurance companies provide premium discounts if this program is used.)
2. *SafeScreen: Screening and Selection Tools for Personnel Managers and Volunteer Coordinators.* Starter kit, $59.95, includes handbook and five applicant packets (file folders with application, release and consent, interview notes, reference checks, W-4, I-9, etc.)
3. *Nexcheck Background Checking Services for Volunteers and Employees.* Cost is per report ordered. Five levels of checks are available: identity verification, address history, statewide criminal history, sex offender registry check, national criminal database history.

NLS Specialties, Inc., P.O. Box 1877, Kennesaw, GA 30156; 770-422-7867; www.nlsspecialties.com. Sells "Kiddie Keepers" security tags and other systems, including stickers, cards, bracelets, and tokens. Also sells emergency evacuation backpacks, diaper bag tags, smocks, custom imprints, etc.

Protecting Our Church and Children: What Church Leaders Must Know, Preschool and Children's Ministry, Baptist State convention of North Carolina, P.O. Box 1107, Cary, NC 27512-1107; 919-467-5100; www.ncbaptist.org. Print 32-page booklet free from Web site or order for $10. Includes information on safety, security, hygiene, policies, sample forms, etc.

Protection Series (14 free booklets on liability risks), Church Mutual Insurance Company, P.O. Box 357, 3000 Schuster Lane, Merrill WI 54452; 800-554-2652; www.churchmutual.com. Series (via mail or printed from Web site) includes child abuse prevention, fire safety, playground safety, transportation, etc. Free sample screening and consent forms (from Joy Melton's book Safe Sanctuaries) are also on Web site, as well as several free videos and Reducing the Risk II Kit at a reduced cost of $15 for customers or $18 for non-customers.

Reducing the Risk II Kit, Christian Ministry Resources, P.O. Box 2600, Big Sandy, TX 75755; 600-222-1840; www.ChurchLawToday.com. Cost is $49.95 for DVD, book, and training manual on screening, hiring, and supervising workers with children.

Safe Sanctuaries: Reducing the Risk of Child Abuse in the Church, by Joy Melton (Nashville: Discipleship Resources, 2004) $13; ISBN 0881772208. Outlines strategies for churchwide plan to recruit, screen, and hire workers; includes sample policies and forms.